S0-ARO-665

Malibu's Cooking Again

A Benefit for Malibu Firestorm Survivors

Edited by Cathy Rogers

*Photography by Robert Duron
and Linda Weldon Conrad*

Cover Art by Laddie John Dill

Copyright © 1995 by Malibu's Cooking Again.

All rights reserved. No portion of this book may be reproduced by any means without prior written permission from the publisher.

Printed in the United States of America
First Edition 1995

Library of Congress
Cataloging-in-Publication Data

Rogers, Cathy, Editor
[Malibu's Cooking Again]
/Cathy Rogers, Editor;
Photography by Robert Duron and
    Linda Weldon Conrad.
Cover art by Laddie John Dill
Includes index.
ISBN 0-9644695-0-2

1. Cooking. 2. Disaster Recovery.
I. Rogers, Cathy, Editor. II. Title.
III. Title: Malibu's Cooking Again.

10 9 8 7 6 5 4

The Image Maker Publishing Company
29417 Bluewater Road
Malibu, CA 90265

This book is dedicated to all those who experienced great losses during the November 1993 firestorms. Your courage is an inspiration to us all.

We would like to thank our BOOK SPONSORS listed below, our PAGE SPONSORS shown on recipe pages inside the book, and the following FRIENDS of *Malibu's Cooking Again* for helping to make this cookbook become a reality.

BOOK SPONSORS:

MALIBU BAY COMPANY
Chabad of Malibu
Greater Malibu Disaster
    Recovery Project
Bette Herson

The Image Maker
    Publishing Company
Jeff & Cathy Rogers
Burton & Charlene Sperber
Jerry & Arlene Waxman

FRIENDS:

Bill & Barbara Adams
Ann Cornelia Andes
Herve & Cecilia Babineau
Thea Brodkin
Mary Ann Cappello

Chandler Design
Mark & Roz Jason
Mark & Susie Johnson
John L. Sundahl

"A good meal in troubled times is always
that much salvaged from disaster."
-- A.J. Liebling

Book design and production by *The Image Maker Publishing Company* and *Malibu's Cooking Again*, Malibu, California.

Editorial production and food styling by Cathy Rogers.

Photographic art direction by Linda Weldon Conrad.

Cover: "Rambla Pacifico" © 1989 by Laddie John Dill. Artist Laddie John Dill translates nature's larger themes into visual metaphors for the Earth's basics: geology, oceans, the ebb and flow of tides and streams, the telling effects of time. His works relate more to the cyclical forces which alter our world than to moments of individual experience.

Contents

Introduction

The fire which blazed through the Santa Monica Mountains on November 2, 1993 destroyed more than 400 homes. For fire victims and bystanders alike, the devastation was unnerving and brought into question our connections with community and the natural elements. It's been a tough year, filled with earthquakes and floods as well. We got through it, and the rebuilding process has begun.

In all the suffering that has gone on, it is impossible to avoid the basic question: Why do we live here? Why, when far away, do we long to get back? Why do we go on, despite mudslides, landslides, danger, and sheer inconvenience?

We know full well that to everything there is a season, and a potential for disaster lurks in every purpose under heaven.

We have seen our share of disasters: the fires this time were inevitable, cyclical, natural. The floods, too, which transformed our ill-paved streets back into the river beds that they were originally intended to be, they too, were predictable. Twenty years ago, this series of fire, earthquake, and flood once again beset the area we are told. This knowledge comforts us in the face of things we cannot control.

This is what we know: There is no personal animus in nature, no hierarchy of one region over another. No vengeful God has it "in" for Malibu, any more than for St. Louis with its floods or Miami with its hurricanes or New York with you name it. A neutral deity merely recognizes the truth of the saying, "Man plans, and God laughs".

It is important to remember, in times of tragedy: Malibu's yellow poppies on a field of green in spring; fall's long clean expanse of quiet empty beach; winter's thundering waves, its moon on the ocean and brilliant sunrise; and summer's smogless heat, the shade of the coral tree, the ride up the coast at sunset, far away from the crowds.

To live here, you come to like being reminded of the truth of man's place in the grand scheme of things. It's a great leveler, knowing that no matter how big we build our homes, how earthquake-proof our foundations, we are fragile dwellers here, temporary residents with movable mailboxes, alongside the coyote, the fawn, the dolphin and the hawk--renters all, in a habitat we can never truly own.

-- *Marlene Marks*

The Kindness Within

It has been said that Nature is neither cruel nor kind: it merely is. And yet the force which has brought Nature into existence and gives it the power to exist, with all its impersonal laws, is kindness itself. We are fragile beings, living in a fragile universe fraught with predators and potential disasters of many kinds. This is our nature and the nature of our world. When a tragedy occurs, our tendency is to see only chaos and agony. "Why?" we ask. But if we can step back for a moment and look with the eyes of passing time, it is possible to catch a glimpse of the kindness which sustains us, giving us another day, healing us, helping us.

One day a madman, in his frustration, lights a fire and downwind a conflagration of frightening proportions races over a mountain range, quickly consuming entire neighborhoods, precious flora and fauna, even people we know by name. Tragedy.

Firefighters, men and women who don't even live here, boldly risk their lives in an attempt to stop the hungry inferno's advance. Friends, neighbors, even complete strangers find themselves bravely rescuing people, homes, pets and possessions. Shelters are set up to house those who have been evacuated. The injured are treated. The community has come alive, shedding all differences to help one another cope with this catastrophe. Healing has already begun. Kindness.

Yesterday, perhaps, the beach bum looked up in envy at the millionaire's mansion on the hill, wishing he had that man's money. The millionaire, perhaps, looked down in envy at the beach bum, wishing he had such a simple life. Today they are side by side, oblivious of station and status, working together to save the place they both call home. Maybe they will stop and share a bit of the inevitable humor, so kindly built into our makeup for use in just this sort of situation. Healing. Kindness.

As the smoke clears, surviving inhabitants hang banners from their balconies, crudely fashioned with whatever they have, but bearing an unmistakably heartfelt message of thanks to the firefighters who saved their homes. People who days ago may have had nothing to say to one another, now smile, laugh, and perhaps cry together, sharing their stories of survival and salvation. Some have suffered tremendous loss, but many others have risen to the occasion, giving, helping, comforting, encouraging. Hearts have been touched, gratitude is felt. The tragedy which might have destroyed us all has somehow brought out the best in us.

The kindness within has asserted itself and faith has been restored.

-- *Alan Roettinger*

Appetizers

one generator
gasoline
jumper cables
"Quick Start"®
electric teapot
coffee cup
paper towels
drip grind coffee
coffee filters

DISASTER RECOVERY COFFEE

1) Check generator for gasoline.
2) Park car by generator and get jumper cables.
3) Start generator, spraying with "Quick Start"® if necessary.
4) Plug in electric teapot. Start water heating in teapot.
5) Wipe coffee cup clean with paper towel.
6) Place coffee filter directly over cup. Put in the coffee grounds.
7) When water is hot, pour over coffee grounds. Do this slowly even though the noise of the generator is loud and irritating.
8) Unplug teapot and turn off generator.
9) Carefully remove wet filter from coffee cup, squeeze out remaining coffee (Caution: this is hot) and discard filter.
10) Pull up a chair under your favorite tree and enjoy!

Don May

GRANITA RESTAURANT'S TEMPURA OF CALAMARI AND BABY VEGETABLES

Combine flour, paprika, salt and pepper in a mixing bowl. Whisk in the soda water gradually until batter is smooth.

Prepare the avocado glaze:

Place avocados, shallots, garlic, herbs, and jalapeño in blender. Add liquids, blending until mixture is an even consistency. Strain and reserve until needed.

Heat oil in a deep-fryer or large pot to 375°. Season squid with salt and pepper. Toss squid and vegetables in flour until coated. Dip squid, then vegetables, in tempura batter and drop immediately into hot oil. Cook until golden brown, about 2 to 3 minutes. Drain on a paper towel.

Toss greens with a small amount of the glaze. Mound in the center of 6 serving plates. Place calamari and vegetables around the greens, and drizzle glaze over. Serve immediately. Serves 6

Chef Kevin Ripley
Granita Restaurant
Malibu

2 pounds fresh cleaned squid
1 pound assorted baby
    vegetables, blanched
all-purpose flour
vegetable or peanut oil for
    deep-frying
mixed baby greens

Tempura batter:
2 cups rice flour
1 teaspoon paprika
1/2 teaspoon kosher salt
1/2 teaspoon cayenne pepper
1 teaspoon white pepper
3 cups soda water

Avocado glaze:
4 ripe avocados, peeled, pitted
    and cut into pieces
2 shallots, peeled and cut in
    pieces
1 clove garlic
1 bunch cilantro, stems removed
1 sprig oregano
1 jalapeño, seeded
1/2 cup lime juice
1 cup orange juice
1/2 cup rice wine vinegar
salt and pepper

This page sponsored by Malibu Bay Company

GEOFFREY'S RESTAURANT EGGPLANT TORTE WITH TOMATO-BASIL SAUCE

2 eggplants
olive oil
2 large white or yellow onions,
    sliced 1/8 inch thick
5 teaspoons fresh garlic, minced
1 shallot, minced
4 bunches fresh spinach, rinsed &
    stems removed
4 large ripe tomatoes, sliced
6 large ripe tomatoes, chopped
1 leek, white part only, chopped
1 cup fresh basil, chopped
few sprigs fresh oregano leaves,
    stems removed
1/2 cup chopped fresh parsley
4 ounces Parmesan cheese,
    grated

1 cup fresh or canned chicken
    stock
1/2 cup white wine
1/4 cup heavy cream
salt and pepper

Slice washed eggplant into 1/4 inch slices, leaving the skin on. Brush with olive oil and lightly grill (or broil) for one minute until lightly browned. Drain on paper towels.

Saute onions in a little olive oil until they wilt, but do not brown. Set aside to cool and drain.

Saute spinach leaves in a little olive oil with the shallot and 1/2 teaspoon of the minced garlic.

Oil a 9" springform pan by wiping some olive oil around the bottom and sides with a paper towel.

Pesto: In a blender or food processor, put 1/2 cup basil, 1/2 cup parsley, 1/2 cup Parmesan cheese and garlic to taste (about 1/2 teaspoon). Blend until smooth. With motor running, slowly add 1/2 cup olive oil in a steady stream until incorporated. Set aside.

Torte: Reserve 6 slices of the eggplant for later. Form a layer on the bottom and sides of the pan with grilled eggplant. Allow the slices to hang over the sides—they'll be folded up and over the top of the torte later.

Make layers of sliced tomatoes, then spinach, then onions and finally pesto on top of the eggplant to cover the bottom of the pan, ending up about halfway up the pan. Continue layering in reverse order: more onions, spinach and then tomatoes on top. Fold over the eggplant slices that were hanging over the edge and add the reserved eggplant slices to totally cover the top of the torte. Wrap entire torte in aluminum foil.

Bake the torte in foil in a 400° oven until heated through, approximately 15 minutes. The entire torte should be refrigerated overnight, and then it will hold together when sliced. Individual slices placed on an oiled cookie pan will heat through in 12 to 15 minutes at 400°.

Sauce: Saute 4 teaspoons of garlic and the leek in a little olive oil until slightly softened. Add the chopped tomatoes, 1/2 cup basil, 1 cup chicken stock, 1/2 cup white wine, 1 teaspoon oregano and salt and pepper to taste. Bring to a boil and simmer 15 to 20 minutes. Puree in a blender and return to the pan. Add 1/4 cup of heavy cream and stir. Set aside.

The torte will serve 8. Each slice should be placed on a pool of 1/2 cup tomato-basil sauce. Serve warmed or at room temperature.

Geoffrey's/Malibu Restaurant

 This page sponsored by Bette Herson

BOO'S PORTOBELLO DELIGHT

10 large Portobello mushrooms,
    stems removed
10 large evenly-sliced slices
    smoked Gouda cheese
10 slices beefsteak tomato

Balsamic Herb Vinaigrette:
1/2 cup balsamic vinegar
1 cup olive oil
1 tablespoon herbs de Provence
1 large clove garlic, crushed
1/2 teaspoon sugar

Heat grill. Brush mushrooms on both sides with vinaigrette. Grill a few minutes on both sides until soft. Turn mushrooms upside down and place a slice of cheese on bottom sides of mushrooms. Place back on the grill and let the cheese melt. Top with slice of tomato, if desired.

Serve with slices of French bread, toasted on the grill. Spread the bread with your choice of mustard, such as Dijon or Pommeroy, and top with the mushrooms.

Beth Jacobson

STUFFED MUSHROOMS

Wash the mushrooms and remove the stems. Grate the Parmesan cheese.

Heat butter and cream cheese in a sauce pan on low heat until melted. Add the grated Parmesan cheese and a pinch of garlic powder and stir.

Place the mushrooms on a cookie sheet and fill with cheese mixture. Bake in a preheated oven at 350° for about 5 to 8 minutes. Serve immediately.

Robert Young
Malibu Colony Gate House

15 to 20 large fresh mushrooms
6 ounces Parmesan cheese (hard wedge)
1/8 pound butter (1/2 stick)
6 ounces Philadelphia cream cheese
garlic powder to taste

CONFETTI DIP

Mix all ingredients. This is delicious as a dip with crackers.

Benita Wilson
Point Dume Project Rebound

2 small cans chopped chilis
1 small can black olives
3 tomatoes, chopped
6 green onions, chopped
chopped parsley
3 avocados, peeled and seeded and chopped
2 tablespoons oil
garlic salt to taste
juice of 1/2 lemon

VALENTINO RESTAURANT'S INVOLTINI DI MELANZANE (WRAPPED EGGPLANTS)

1 large or 2 small eggplants
soy or peanut oil
salt to taste
2 to 3 ounces Caprini cheese
    (or any mild goat cheese)

Dressing:

1 tablespoon mustard
4 drops Worcestershire sauce
2 teaspoons wine vinegar
salt and pepper to taste
bit of minced garlic (optional)

Slice the eggplants into 1/2 inch slices in cutlet shape. Sprinkle a little salt over the slices and let them rest for about 10 minutes so that the natural water drains. Pat dry.

In a very hot skillet, put enough oil so that the dry slices of eggplant will float, 3 or 4 at a time, and cook about 1 minute. Do not overcook! Continue cooking the eggplant slices in this manner, allowing the cooked slices to rest on a paper or cloth towel. When all slices are cooked, place them on a large platter.

Cut the Caprini cheese in 1 inch squares (about 1 large table-spoon) and place one in the center of each eggplant slice.

Roll the eggplant around the cheese like a cigarette.

Whisk dressing ingredients in a bowl quickly.

Gently pour the dressing over the eggplant and let them marinate in the refrigerator for about one day.

Valentino Restaurant
Santa Monica

VEGETABLE QUICHE

Spread melted butter on the pie shell and bake until it begins to brown.

Sauté the onions and mushrooms, and add to the cooked vegetables. Mix mayonnaise, eggs, flour, milk, and cheese. Add to the vegetable mixture. Pour into the baked pie shell and bake pie at 375° for 45 minutes or until brown. Serves 6 to 8.

Bruce Konheim

1 deep pie shell

1/2 cup chopped onions
1 cup sliced mushrooms

1 package frozen vegetables,
    any type, cooked and drained

1/3 cup mayonnaise
2 eggs
2 tablespoons flour
1/2 cup milk
8 ounces Cheddar cheese, grated

TROPICAL SANGRIA

Place all ingredients in a large pitcher and serve immediately. For a visua as well as a sensual treat, make the tea by the package directions, but leave out 2 cups of water. Pour all ingredients into a large pitcher and stir in a dozen or more ice cubes. Serve immediately.

Paradise Tropical Tea Co.

1 orange, quartered
1 lime, quartered
1/2 gallon Paradise Tropical Tea,
    brewed according to package
    directions and cooled
2 cups soda water
1 teaspoon sugar
Sliced kiwi and/or pineapple

 This page sponsored by Café Au Lait, Inc.

TAVERNA TONY RESTAURANT'S
TARAMOSALATA (GREEK CAVIAR DIP)

1/2 pound Greek red caviar
1/2 pound white bread, soaked
   in water
1/2 pound olive oil
2 lemons, juiced
1 red onion, chopped

Place onions, red caviar, and lemon juice in food processor. Blend for 30 seconds.

Squeeze the soaked bread until dry. Add bread to caviar and onion mixture in food processor. Blend for 10 seconds.

Add olive oil slowly while blending until the desired richness and consistency in mixture is reached.

Serve with pita bread as an appetizer to share, garnished with olive oil, paprika, parsley, and Kalamata olives. Optional: sprinkle with salmon caviar.

Serves 10.

Antony Koursaris
Taverna Tony Restaurant
Malibu

Soups, Salads & Vegetables

"I dragged the SCUBA gear, the cat, and my body to the edge of our neighbor's pool. The sky up the hill was now bright orange. I decided that a cat that had dodged owls, hawks, bobcats, and coyotes for 14 years didn't need my advice. Freed, he bounded to a fence and watched the orange 'thing'. As I was checking the SCUBA gear, a 20 foot palm tree next to the pool exploded like a Roman candle, showering me with sparks. Three smaller ones across the pool went off in sequence like some 4th of July fireworks stunt. It didn't seem that hot but I had definitely underestimated how much time I had. The firestorm had grown in size to a level where it now generated its own wind. As it came down the hill toward the ocean, a noise like a freight train surrounded me. It seemed like my signal to stumble gracefully into the deep end with tank, regulator, and 20 lbs. of weights to keep me on the bottom.

After 25 minutes I surfaced and tried the smoky air. With a wet T-shirt tied across my face, I could breathe. All around me looked like Hell was supposed to look. The houses across the street with shake shingle roofs had burned to the ground in less than 25 minutes. We were extremely fortunate in losing only 2 cars and most of our landscaping. Our son Chris, with a cool head through it all, helped several others escape down the arroyo, including carrying a barefoot 80 year old lady down to the Pacific Coast Highway. He knew it would be close, but he beat the firestorm by less than 3 minutes, as it then ate the arroyo. One of our neighbors watched from the PCH in shock as Chris emerged. Garfield later appeared unsinged."

-- Mike Gleason

GAZPACHO

3 large ripe tomatoes, skinned
1/2 large cucumber, peeled and
    seeded and cut into pieces
1/2 large green pepper, seeded
    and cut into pieces
1 small or medium onion, peeled
    and cut into pieces
1 large clove garlic, peeled
3 tablespoons wine vinegar
white pepper or Tabasco®
    Sauce to taste

Cut the tomatoes in pieces and place in blender. Blend briefly, then add the cucumber, green pepper, onion, garlic, vinegar and pepper. Blend with an on-and-off motion until soup is of desired consistency. Longer blending will result in a thinner soup. Chill well before serving.

Serves 4

Joanne Jacobson

"WARMS YOUR HEART" FRUIT SOUP

7 cups water
1 cup orange juice
4 fresh D'Anjou pears, diced
1 cup raisins
1 cup dried apricots, quartered
1/2 cup pitted prunes, quartered
1 tablespoon grated orange rind
1 teaspoon cinnamon
1/4 teaspoon nutmeg
whipped cream
fresh mint

Fix this special soup for a holiday breakfast while you prepare your main meal and it will fill your house with the delicious aroma of cinnamon and fruit.

Heat water, juice and raisins just to boiling. Add pears, spices, and the other fruits. Reduce heat and simmer for 30-45 minutes, or until pears are cooked and soup has thickened a bit. Add whipped cream, a dusting of cinnamon, and a sprig of mint just before serving for a festive touch.

Bev Hammond

16

Shown in the photo in front is Granita Restaurant's
"Tempura of Calamari and Baby Vegetables",
accompanied by the restaurant's "Crisp Potato Galette
with Gravlax and Dill Creme Fraiche" and "Maine
"Crabcakes with Smoky Red Pepper Sauce".

MOONSHADOWS RESTAURANT CLAM CHOWDER

Place clams, clam juice, potatoes, leeks, celery, bell peppers, onion, clam base, Lea & Perrins®, Tabasco®, and pepper into a large stock pot and bring to a boil.

When the mixture has started to boil, melt butter slowly in a separate pot. Do not burn. When butter is liquified, add the flour and stir until completely dissolved into a thick roux. Slowly add the milk and the 1/2 & 1/2 and stir together well. Continue to stir until the mixture has thickened and just starts to bubble.

Add this mixture to the boiling clam mixture and stir well. Bring back almost to a boil.

Important: After removing from the heat, the soup must be stirred frequently as it cools or it will separate. Serves 8-10.

Moonshadows Restaurant
Malibu

3 pounds chopped clams,
   shells removed
1 quart clam juice
1 pound diced raw potatoes
1 large leek, diced
2 stalks celery, diced
1 bell pepper, diced
1/2 spanish onion, diced
1 ounce clam base
1/2 ounce Lea & Perrins®
   Worcestershire sauce
3 drops Tabasco®
1 teaspoon black pepper

1 quart 1/2 & 1/2
1 cup all purpose flour
12 tablespoons butter

ITALIAN STYLE CHOWDER

1/2 pound zucchini, sliced
2 onions, sliced
1 15-ounce can garbanzo beans
1 1-pound can tomatoes,
    chopped
1/4 cup butter or margarine
1 1/2 cups dry white wine
2 teaspoons minced garlic
1 teaspoon minced basil leaves
1 bay leaf
salt and pepper to taste
1 cup shredded Jack cheese
1 cup grated Romano cheese
1 cup whipping cream or
    half-and-half

Combine the zucchini, onions, beans, tomatoes and their liquid, butter, wine, garlic, basil, and bay leaf in a 3-quart baking dish.

Cover and bake at 400° for 1 hour, stirring once halfway through. Season to taste with salt and pepper.

Stir in cheeses and cream. Bake 10 minutes longer. Makes three quarts. Any chowder left over can be frozen.

Jeff and Sherri Kramer

THE GREEN SOUP

This recipe was taught to me by my mother. Our family always enjoys it. I will get a phone call from one of five brothers and sisters and usually in the course of the conversation, one of us will say, "Guess what's cooking?" And we always know it's the Green Soup!

Eighteen days after the fire came the birth of our son Darian. When I came home to our temporary home, a familiar smell greeted me at the door: Green Soup! What a great feeling—Green Soup at just the right time! My husband was the cook that time.

1 1/2 cups green split peas *
1/2 cup yellow split peas *
2 quarts water
1 lamb shank or short ribs
1/2 onion, chopped
1 parsnip, chopped
1 cup celery, chopped
1 cup carrots, chopped
1 bay leaf, crumbled

* Soak peas overnight

Boil the peas in the water for 1 hour. Add the vegetables and shank or ribs and bring to a boil. Slowly simmer for 2 1/2 to 3 hours, stirring often. Salt and pepper to taste before serving.

Nasser and Marla Abari

 This page sponsored by the Abari family

SUMMER GARDEN SOUP

8 cups water
8 inches dried Kombu seaweed
5-6 shiitaki mushrooms
1 cup carrots sliced diagonally
2 cups daikon radish cut in
   crescents
1 small head broccoli, separated
   into florets
3 stems of broccoli, peeled
   and sliced
1 teaspoon lemon juice
1 thin slice of lemon
1/2 teaspoon sea salt
1/2 cup tamari

Make stock using 8 cups of water, 8 inches dried kombu seaweed* cut in 1/2 inch squares, and 5 to 6 dried shiitake mushrooms. Bring to a boil. After mushrooms have softened, remove them, cut stems off, dice remaining coarsely and return to stock.

Cut carrots in thin diagonal slices. Cut daikon radish into crescents by first cutting in 1/4 inch rounds, then cut in half. Separate broccoli head into bite-sized florets. Peel the fiber from broccoli stems and cut the stalks crosswise every 1 1/2 inches and then cut each piece lengthwise 2-3 times.

Add to stock the cut carrots, daikon, broccoli florets and stems, lemon slice and lemon juice. Cook over medium heat for 10 minutes.

Near the end of the cooking time, add 1/2 teaspoon sea salt and 1/2 cup tamari. Serves 6 to 8

*Kombu seaweed is a basic ingredient for making stocks for Japanese-style soup. The salty white powder that adheres to the leaves is full of flavor and should not be washed off. It has a long shelf life and can be found at Oriental markets or some health food stores.

Bev Hammond

THE GODMOTHER'S VEGETABLE SOUP WITH BASIL AND PINE NUTS (MINESTRONE CON BASILICO E PINOLI)

The onion, 1 carrot and 1 stalk of celery should be chopped very finely and added to 2/3 cup of olive oil in a large pot. Fry gently over low heat until golden. Add remaining vegetables and water to cover completely. Bring to a boil and reduce to medium heat for about 20 minutes, or until the carrots are tender. Add the beans and heat thoroughly.

Pesto

Mix the basil, garlic, pine nuts, butter, and 2/3 cup olive oil in a blender until pureed. Add a good handful of Parmesan cheese.

When the vegetables are cooked, remove the soup from the stove and stir in the pesto. Serve the soup with the remaining olive oil and Parmesan Cheese.

Serves 6

The Godmother Restaurant
Malibu

1 large onion
3 peeled carrots
3 celery stalks
1 3/4 cup extra-virgin olive oil
salt* to taste
1/4 shredded cabbage
5 zucchini
5 potatoes, peeled and diced
1 leek, sliced and well rinsed
1 spring onion (scallion) sliced
1 1/2 cups cooked cannellini
    beans
5 small bunches fresh basil
1 cup pine nuts
7 tablespoons unsalted butter,
    softened
8 ounces Regglano Parmesan
    cheese, finely grated

*Salt is optional. The God-mother Restaurant does not use salt in any of their cooking.

 This page sponsored by Ellen & Douglas Weitman

3 tablespoons butter
1 leek, white part only
2 stalks celery, chopped
1 onion, chopped
1 pound beef stew meat, cubed
4 cups chicken broth
1/3 cup barley
1/4 cup chopped fresh parsley
1 bay leaf
1/2 teaspoon thyme
salt & pepper to taste
1 potato, diced
1 cup light cream

HEARTY BEEF, LEEK AND BARLEY STEW

Melt the butter in a large pot. Saute leek, celery, onion, and meat over low heat, stirring occasionally for about 20 minutes. Add broth and barley. Bring to a boil. Add parsley, bay leaf, thyme, salt and pepper. Cover and simmer about 2 hours. Add potato. Cover and simmer about 30 to 40 minutes. Remove bay leaf and stir in the cream. Heat until warm, about 5 minutes.

Ellen Weitman

MILK TOAST

1 piece of white bread
1 cup very hot milk
Soft butter
Sugar

This is sort of the "white bread" version of chicken soup, and works just as well! It's interesting that they are both fairly oily. It's great for anyone, but kids always love it. Mom always served us this when we kids were home sick-- we considered it a great treat.

Toast the bread. Spread butter very freely and liberally on the toast. Put the toast into a cereal or soup bowl and sprinkle some sugar freely over it. Heat the milk to a strong simmer, and pour it over the toast, covering it.

Push the now floating toast down a few times until it stays down, and the butter begins to melt and mix into the milk.

Katherine Price & Bonnie Porter

This page sponsored by Katherine Price

SALMON-CUCUMBER SPA SALAD

Wash salmon. Place in a fish poacher and add just enough water to cover. Add sliced lemon, peppercorns, bay leaf and celery tops, and salt. Slowly bring to a boil, then reduce heat and simmer, covered, for 30 to 35 minutes.

Carefully lift salmon out of water onto a plate. Let stand until cool enough to handle, then remove skin and bones. (There should be about 2 1/2 pounds of fish remaining) Break the fish into large chunks in a large bowl. Chill several hours.

Make the dressing by combining all ingredients, mixing well. Refrigerate 1 hour.

Just before serving, toss the salmon and dressing. Taste for salt. Add if needed.

To serve, line a large serving plate with lettuce. Mound fish in the middle and garnish with tomato and lemon wedges and cucumber slices.

Serves 12

Vicki Cooper
Faces & Legs by Vicki

Salad:

3 1/2 pound piece fresh salmon
1/2 lemon, sliced
6 whole black peppercorns
1 bay leaf
tops from 2 stalks of celery
salt to taste

Dressing:

1 1/2 cups mayonnaise or salad
    dressing
1 1/2 tablespoons lemon juice
3 tablespoons fresh snipped dill
1 1/2 cups diced pared cucumber

Boston or iceberg lettuce
tomato wedges
lemon wedges
cucumber slices

DILL PASTA SALAD

2 cups mostaccioli noodles

1/2 cup sliced baby carrots
1/2 cup broccoli florets
1/4 cup butter

1/4 cup sliced shallots
1 teaspoon crushed garlic
1 tablespoon chopped fresh
    parsley
1 tablespoon chopped fresh dill
1/2 cup water packed artichoke
    hearts, quartered lengthwise
1/4 cup olive oil
1/3 cup rice vinegar

2 ounces fresh Parmesan cheese,
    grated

1/2 teaspoon paprika

Boil mostaccioli to just past al dente, rinse in a colander with cool water and set aside.

While the pasta is boiling, slightly saute the carrots and broccoli in the butter, and add to the mostaccioli.

In a small mixing bowl, combine shallots, garlic, parsley, dill, artichoke hearts, oil, and vinegar. Pour the contents of the mixing bowl over the mostaccioli, carrots and broccoli, and toss the mixture, coating the mostaccioli completely. Add the Parmesan cheese, and toss again. Place in the refrigerator to cool for half an hour.

When ready to serve, place in shallow salad bowls or plates and garnish with the paprika.

Lieutenant Mike Moore
Lost Hills/Malibu Sheriff's Station

CARROTS RESTAURANT'S CHICKEN SALAD

Sauté chicken. Cool. Cut the cooled chicken and the lettuce in thin slices.

Cut the bottom off the kaiware and enoki mushrooms. Mix the chicken, lettuce, and enoki mushrooms.

Mix vinegar with the egg yolk. Add the oil and then all other ingredients. Pour on dressing and gently blend.

Place salad on three plates and place kaiware on top. You may add roasted pine nuts if desired. Serves three.

Carrots Restaurant
Santa Monica

1/4 chicken, skinned & boned
1/8 head iceberg lettuce
1/2 package kaiware (radish
   sprouts)
1/2 package enoki mushrooms
roasted pine nuts (optional)

Dressing:

1/4 cup vinegar
1 egg yolk
1/2 cup sesame oil
2 teaspoons dry chinese mustard
2 teaspoons soy sauce
salt and pepper to taste

DUCK DUCK MOUSSE'S ROASTED NEW POTATO AND SAUSAGE SALAD

14 new potatoes, sliced
1/4 cup olive oil
salt and pepper to taste
1 pound linguica (Portuguese
   garlic sausage)
2 cups collard greens, cut in thin
   strips (arugula may be
   substituted)
3/4 cup hazelnuts, roasted and
   coarsely chopped
2 cups sweet red peppers,
   julienned
1/2 bunch green onions, diced
1/2 cup Kalamata olives, seeded
   and sliced
chili mayonnaise

Chili mayonnaise:
juice of one lemon
1 tablespoon Dijon mustard
1 egg
salt and pepper to taste
1 1/2 cups basil or garlic flavored
   olive oil
Chili puree:
2 tablespoons olive oil
1 tablespoon minced dried pasilla
   chili or achiote
1 shallot, peeled & chopped
2 cloves garlic, peeled & chopped

Toss potato slices with oil. Place potatoes on a baking sheet and sprinkle with salt and pepper. Bake at 450° for 40 minutes, stirring occasionally. Set aside to cool.

While potatoes are roasting, gently poach linguica in small amount of water for 20 minutes. Drain well, then grill, turning often, until well-browned and crisp. Cool and slice thinly.

Combine potatoes, linguica, collard greens, hazelnuts, sweet red peppers, and olives. Add chili mayonnaise to taste.

For chili mayonnaise, place first five ingredients in a Cuisinart and blend. After five seconds, pour oil in a thin stream through feed tube while machine is running until mayonnaise thickens.

Make chili puree by heating oil in a small saucepan, then stir in chili, shallot, and garlic. Sauté until soft. Remove from heat and puree in a small food processor or food mill.

Add chili puree to mayonnaise mixture, blending well, then toss with salad ingredients.   Makes 12 to 14 servings.

Aleta Parrish
Duck Duck Mousse at The Victorian
Santa Monica

MARMALADE CAFÉ'S THAI NOODLE SALAD

Cook the spaghetti, drain and toss with 2 tablespoons of the vegetable oil and set aside.

Heat sesame oil. Toast the sesame seeds lightly in this oil, being careful not to burn them. Remove from fire when lightly toasted, as they will continue to cook in hot oil.

Combine seeds in sesame oil with the remaining vegetable oil, rice vinegar, coriander, soy sauce, chili flakes and garlic.

Toss sauce with the spaghetti, carrots, chives or scallions, cilantro, and peanuts. Chill, or serve at room temperature.

Marmalade Café
Malibu

1 pound spaghetti
3 large carrots, julienned
2 bunches chives, chopped, or 1
   bunch scallions, chopped
1/2 bunch cilantro, chopped
1 cup peanuts, left whole and
   roasted (no skins)

Sauce:

1 1/2 cups vegetable oil
2 1/2 tablespoons sesame oil
2 tablespoons sesame seeds
1/2 cup seasoned rice vinegar
3 tablespoons ground coriander
3/4 cup soy sauce
1 tablespoon red chili flakes
4 cloves garlic, chopped

This page sponsored by Eileen Dunne Zell

BROWN DERBY RESTAURANT COBB SALAD

1/2 head iceberg lettuce
1/2 bunch Romaine lettuce
1 bunch watercress
1 bunch parsley
2 medium tomatoes, peeled,
    seeded and diced
6 strips bacon, cooked until crisp
    and crumbled into pieces
2 cooked chicken breasts, cut
    into small pieces
1 avocado, cut into small pieces
3 hard-cooked eggs, chopped
2 tablespoons chopped chives
1/2 cup finely grated imported
    Roquefort cheese

Brown Derby Old Fashioned
French Dressing:
1 cup water
1 cup red wine vinegar
1 teaspoon sugar
Juice of 1 lemon
2 1/2 teaspoons salt
1 tablespoon ground black pepper
1 tablespoon Worcestershire
    sauce
1 tablespoon English mustard
1 clove garlic, chopped
1 cup olive oil
3 cups canola oil

For dressing, blend all ingredients except oils in blender or food processor. Slowly add the oils. Mix well. Chill and shake thoroughly before serving on salad.

Cut lettuces, watercress and parsley into bite-size pieces and place in salad bowl. Arrange tomatoes, bacon and chicken pieces on top of the salad and arrange the chopped avocado around the edge of the salad. Sprinkle the top of the salad with eggs, chives, and cheese, and toss with 1 cup of the dressing just before serving.

Peggy Cobb
Brown Derby Restaurant

CAESAR SALAD WRAPPED IN CUCUMBER

For Caesar dressing, combine all ingredients except oil in blender or food processor. With motor running, slowly pour in oil. Place in a jar and refrigerate until ready to use.

For beet vinaigrette, place all ingredients except oil in blender or food processor. With motor running, slowly pour in oil. Place in a squeeze bottle and refrigerate until ready to use.

Brush lettuce leaves with Caesar dressing, and reserve the remainder of the dressing. Place 3 to 5 leaves of Romaine together and wrap with cucumber slices inside. Secure with a toothpick. Make a total of 6 bunches. Cut the bottoms of the bunches so that they will stand up on the plates.

Place the bunches upright on the plates. Place a little Caesar dressing on each side, and squeeze a small amount of the beet vinaigrette in the center of the dressing. Dust with Parmesan cheese and freshly ground pepper to taste. Garnish with julienned beet.

Try serving the Pizza with Ratatouille along with this salad instead of croutons.

Serves 6

Cathy Rogers

Caesar dressing:
1 egg white
5 flat anchovies
3 cloves garlic
1/2 tablespoon English mustard
1/4 cup red wine vinegar
1/4 cup water
1 tablespoon Dijon mustard
pinch cayenne pepper
juice of 1/2 lemon
2 teaspoons sugar
2 teaspoons Worcestershire
    sauce
1 cup canola oil

6 thin vertical slices hothouse
    cucumbers
30 pieces romaine lettuce leaves,
    washed and wrapped in a
    paper towel to dry
12 toothpicks

Beet vinaigrette:
1 cooked beet, peeled
2 cloves garlic
2 teaspoon sugar
1 teaspoons dry mustard
2 teaspoons Dijon mustard
1 teaspoons Worcestershire sauce
1 cup canola oil
1/2 cup Parmesan cheese, grated
freshly ground pepper
1 beet, peeled and julienned

29

ZENZERO RESTAURANT GRILLED SCALLION MARINATED SHRIMP SALAD

Garlic oil:
1 head garlic
1 cup peanut oil

Shrimp:
20 medium shrimp
1 bunch scallions, minced
3 cloves garlic, minced
1/2 teaspoon crushed red chilis
1 to 2 tablespoons peanut oil
salt and black pepper to taste

Tahini dressing:
1/2 tablespoon shiro (white)
   miso *
2 tablespoons tahini*
1 tablespoon soy sauce
1/2 cup rice wine vinegar
1 1/2 cups peanut oil
salt and black pepper to taste
* Available in health food stores

Salad:
4 to 5 leaves red cabbage
3 heads baby frisee
1 hothouse cucumber
3 ounces tahini dressing
salt and black pepper to taste

For the garlic oil, break the head of garlic into cloves, leaving the skin on but discarding the outer layers. Drizzle the cloves with 1 tablespoon of the oil and roast them in a 325° oven until they are soft all the way through. This may take over 1 hour. After they have cooled, peel away the skin with a small knife. Pour the remaining oil over the garlic and let it sit for at least 2 days. Afterwards, the garlic may be kept in the oil as a garnish or strained out.

Peel and devein the shrimp, leaving the tail intact. Chop the scallions, garlic, and red chilis together. Toss the mixture with the shrimp and a little oil to moisten. Let this marinate 8 to 12 hours in the refrigerator.

For the tahini dressing, place the miso, tahini, soy sauce and rice wine vinegar together in a blender. Turn it on low and begin emulsifying in the peanut oil. If done properly, a funnel will form and close just as the last of the oil is added. Season with salt and black pepper.

Lay the red cabbage leaves atop each other, roll them up like a cigar, and then julienne them. The red cabbage must be washed off until it no longer bleeds purple, and then drained.

Peel the cucumber and discard the skin. Keep on peeling it to the core and drop the peelings into ice water so they stay crisp.

Wash the frisee and chop it into bite-size pieces.

When ready to serve the salad, brush a heated grill with an oil dampened rag. Season the shrimp with salt and black pepper and place them on the grill. While the shrimp are cooking, toss the cabbage, cucumber and frisee with 3 ounces of tahini dressing. Set a mound of salad in the center of each plate and surround it with 5 shrimp. Just before serving the salad, drizzle a little garlic oil over each shrimp.

Serves 4

ZenZero Restaurant
Santa Monica

PATIO GARDEN SALAD

A selection of whatever salad greens you may have from your garden: lettuce, watercress, raddichio, hearts of palm, sprouts, chives, parsley, etc.

Today's pick of any edible, non-poisonous patio flowers to add to the salad: geraniums, violets, pansies, violas, rose, nasturtiums, alyssum, squash, cucumber, or daylily.

The flowers of various garden herbs will also add a spicy flavor and a distinctive taste.

<u>Dressing:</u> One part fresh lemon juice to one part sugar or honey.

This salad was a favorite of Rosemary and O.P. Reed before the firestorm burned their home and garden on Seagull Dr.

In a large bowl, arrange washed and dried salad greens.

Now go out to your garden and look for any of the following flowers: Geraniums of any color; violets (should you be so lucky), or pansies or violas. Nasturtiums are a wonderful addition to salads, both leaves and flowers. Alyssum is ubiquitous and many people do not think of it as an edible flower, but actually a few blossom tufts added to the salad give a burst of flavor, similar to radish. The flowers of thyme, marjoram, rosemary, lavender, parsley, chives, and celery are delicious. And do not forget the rose. It is a paradigm of perfection in the salad. Any non-poisonous blossoms are candidates for the salad. Do not overlook the squash and cucumber blossoms in season. Daylilies, bought at premium prices in the Oriental market are used in Oriental cooking. Use them fresh from your garden.

Arrange the flowers on and around the salad greens.

Dress with: One part fresh lemon juice to one part sugar or honey (to taste). Or combine half mayonnaise and half sour cream, adding herbs and vinegar, mustard, cayenne or sugar to heighten taste.

Rosemary Reed

Shown in the photo top left is "Caesar Salad Wrapped in Cucumber" and "Pizza With Ratatouille of Vegetables", ZenZero Restaurant's "Grilled Scallion Marinated Shrimp Salad", and in front, Primi Restaurant's "Involtini di Swordfish and Shrimp" with a Parmesan potato chip.

MICHAEL'S RESTAURANT CHICKEN GOAT CHEESE SALAD

Bone 6 chicken breast halves, leaving skin on and wing bones attached.

Cut 1 log (about 12 ounces) of fresh, creamy white California goat cheese into 1/4-inch medallions.

Cut red and yellow bell peppers into 3/4 to 1 inch wide strips.

Peel onion and cut into 3/8-inch slices. Set all above ingredients aside while you make the Tomato Cancasse, Balsamic Vinaigrette, and the Jalapeño-Cilantro-Lime Salsa.

Combine all ingredients of the Tomato Cancasse, cover and chill in the refrigerator for at least 30 minutes.

To make the Balsamic Vinaigrette, place all ingredients except oil in blender or food processor. Blend, while slowly adding oil. Refrigerate until needed.

Combine all ingredients of the Jalapeño-Cilantro-Lime Salsa and set aside until needed. (Recipe follows Vinaigrette)

This recipe continues on the following page.

6 chicken breast halves
1 log (12 ounces) goat cheese
salt and freshly ground pepper

3 each red and yellow bell
    peppers, stemmed & seeded
1 large or 2 medium-size Maui,
    Walla Walla, Vidalia, or
    sweet red onions, peeled
2 tablespoons extra-virgin
    olive oil

3 heads limestone lettuce, leaves
    separated, washed, dried,
    and torn
3 bunches mache, leaves
    separated, washed, dried,
    and torn
2 bunches arugula, leaves
    separated, washed, dried,
    and torn
2 heads baby red leaf lettuce,
    leaves separated, washed,
    dried, and torn
1 head baby radicchio, leaves
    separated

1 cup Tomato Concasse
1 cup Balsamic Vinaigrette
1 cup Jalapeño-Cilantro-Lime
   salsa
1 bunch fresh chives, finely
   chopped

Tomato Concasse:
4 medium tomatoes, red or
   yellow, peeled, seeded and
   chopped
1 cup extra virgin olive oil
1/4 cup sherry wine vinegar
1/2 shallot, minced
2 tablespoons julienne of fresh
   basil
sea salt and freshly ground
   pepper to taste

Balsamic Vinaigrette:
1/2 cup balsamic vinegar
1/2 cup water
3 large cloves garlic
2 tablespoons Dijon mustard
2 1/2 tablespoons sugar
2 tablespoons Worcestershire
   sauce
1/4 teaspoon sea salt
freshly ground pepper
2 cups canola oil

To make the salad, first preheat the grill or broiler.

With your finger, gently make a pocket between the skin and meat of each chicken breast, inserting your finger along the long side of each breast and leaving the skin attached along the other edges. Insert the medallions of goat cheese, overlapping slightly, inside the pockets to stuff the chicken breasts. Sprinkle the breasts with salt and pepper.

Brush the red and yellow pepper strips and onion slices with the olive oil and season with salt and pepper. Set aside.

Grill the chicken breasts, skin side up first, until nicely browned, 3 to 5 minutes. Turn them over and grill for 5 to 7 minutes more.

About 1 minute before the chicken is done, place the peppers and onion slices on the grill and grill them about 30 seconds per side, until heated through and lightly charred.

Arrange all the salad leaves on 6 large serving plates.

Cut each grilled breast crosswise into 4 or 5 slices and place in the center of a bed of greens. Garnish each plate with 3 spoonfuls of tomato concasse and the grilled peppers and onions. Dress the vegetables with the vinaigrette. Spoon the salsa over the chicken. Sprinkle each serving with chopped chives.

Serves 6

*Michael's Restaurant
Santa Monica*

Jalapeño-Cilantro-Lime Salsa:

2 medium tomatoes, peeled,
    seeded and diced
1 tablespoon fresh cilantro
    leaves
1/2 jalapeno pepper, seeded
    and diced
juice of 2 limes
1/2 cup olive oil
2 tablespoons sherry wine
    vinegar
sea salt
freshly ground pepper

This page sponsored by Cross Creek
Preservation Co./Duarte Landowners

LOW-FAT COLESLAW

3/4 cup low-fat mayonnaise or
    dressing
3 tablespoons sugar
1 1/2 tablespoons white wine
    vinegar
1/8 teaspoon garlic powder
1/8 teaspoon onion powder
1/8 teaspoon dry mustard
1/8 teaspoon celery salt
dash black pepper
1 tablespoon lemon juice
1/2 cup non-fat sour cream
1/4 teaspoon salt
1 large head cabbage, finely
    shredded

Blend all ingredients except cabbage. Stir until smooth. Pour over the cabbage in a large bowl and toss until cabbage is well coated. Cover and chill until serving time.

Margery McCallister

CUCUMBER SALAD

peeled cucumber
    (1/4 per person)

equal amounts of lemon juice or
    vinegar and water
sugar to taste
big splash vegetable oil
dill weed to taste

Use a potato peeler to slice cucumber into thin length-wise slices. Scoop out seeds and discard as you slice down.

Mix first two ingredients of sauce together until you are satisfied with the sweet/tart taste. Add the oil and dill. Pour over sliced cucumbers and mix well. Refrigerate until fully chilled.

Walt Shirk
Captain/Paramedic, Engine Co. 1, B Platoon
Santa Monica

ANNIE'S BAKED BEANS

We have lived in Malibu for 30 years and have been so close so many times, but have never lost our home. Our hearts go out to all those who did--we love you.

Layer one third of the beans in the bottom of a 13 x 9 1/2 inch oblong baking dish. Sprinkle or drizzle over the beans 1/3 of the brown sugar, molassas, and ketsup. Top with 1/3 of the sliced onions. Repeat this process two more times. Top last layer with slices of lean, raw bacon.

Bake 1 hour at 350° or until bacon is done.

Ann Cornelia Andes (Dixon)

3 large cans B & M Baked Beans,
   with pork fat removed
1 1/2 cups brown sugar
3/4 cup molassas
3/4 cup ketsup
2-3 Spanish onions, thinly sliced
1/2 pound lean bacon, uncooked

BAMBU RESTAURANT'S FRENCH FRIES

Heat the oil to 350°. Combine the seasoning salt ingredients and set aside.

Add the potatoes to the hot oil and cook, stirring a few times, until golden brown. Remove from oil and dab with a paper towel.

Place in a bowl and season with seasoning salt.

Marc Boornazian
Bambu Restaurant/Malibu

2 potatoes, cut julienned
3 cups frying oil

Seasoning Salt:
1/4 teaspoon paprika
pinch of salt
pinch of pepper
1/4 teaspoon chile powder
large pinch of cayenne pepper

WHISKIED CARROTS

1 bunch carrots
2 tablespoons carrot water
3 tablespoons butter
3 tablespoons brown sugar
3 tablespoons Rye whiskey
dash pepper

Peel the carrots and cut lengthwise. Cook in a covered skillet in a small amount of water until tender-crisp. Remove the carrots from the pan.

To the carrot water, add the butter, brown sugar, and pepper. Cook to a heavy syrup. Place carrots in the syrup and cook until glazed, shaking pan. Place in a serving dish. Rinse out the pan with whiskey and pour mixture over the carrots. Serve warm.

Mary Lou Blackwood, Executive V.P.
Malibu Chamber of Commerce

 This page sponsored by the Board of Directors
of the Malibu Chamber of Commerce

CORN DIEGO

Soak the dried Chipotle pepper in just enough warm water to cover it, for 10 minutes.

Roast the Pasilla peppers over the gas flame of a stove or an outdoor grill. Using the outdoor grill to roast the vegetables improves the flavor of the dish. Once the peppers are blackened on the outside, place them in a plastic bag and allow to cool. When cool, peel off the charred skin, and remove veins and seeds. Cut into 1" square pieces.

Roast the tomatoes until blackened. Place in a blender along with the Chipotle pepper and 2 tablespoons of the liquid that the pepper was soaked in. Blend for 5 to 10 seconds.

Heat a saute pan large enough to hold all the ingredients. Add 1 tablespoon olive oil and allow to heat. Add the chopped onion and saute until translucent, then add the garlic. Cook until the garlic begins to turn brown. Add the corn and the Pasilla pepper, and cook on medium heat for 2 minutes. Pour in the contents of the blender and 1 cup of the vegetable broth. Bring to a boil, add the remaining seasonings and reduce heat to a simmer. Cook uncovered on a low simmer for 30 minutes. Add the remaining cup of broth as needed to prevent the mixture from drying out. This dish goes well with Mexican entrees or grilled salmon.

Jim Musante from John's Garden Fresh Health Store Malibu

1 dried Chipotle pepper
2 fresh Pasilla peppers
2 ripe Roma tomatoes
1 tablespoon olive oil
1 medium onion, chopped
1 clove garlic, minced
2 ears of corn, cut off the cob
1 14-ounce can vegetable broth, or 2 cups homemade vegetable broth
1/4 teaspoon ground cumin
1/4 teaspoon salt
1/4 teaspoon chili powder
1/8 teaspoon cayenne pepper (or use black pepper if you want a milder dish)

39

BARBEQUED BUTTER BEANS

2 cups large dried butter beans
medium size piece of salt pork

1 large onion, minced
1 clove garlic, minced
1 1/2 teaspoons chili pepper
1 1/2 tablespoons butter

1 11 1/2 ounce can condensed
    tomato soup
1/4 cup brown sugar
1/4 cup vinegar
1/8 teaspoon black pepper
1 teaspoon prepared mustard
1/2 teaspoon celery seed
1/2 teaspoon salt

Quickly rinse the beans and add to boiling water with salt pork in it. Cook until almost tender, about 40 minutes. Drain and save 1 can (use the tomato soup can) of liquid and the salt pork for the sauce.

Saute the onion, garlic, and chili pepper in butter until tender. Add the soup, sugar, vinegar, black pepper, mustard, celery seed, salt and the can of liquid saved from the beans.

Place the beans in a covered baking dish, and spoon the sauce over them. Place the salt pork on top in a fan shape. Bake in 350o oven about one hour. Remove lid and bake about 15 minutes longer.

Variations: White beans may be substituted. Brown pinto beans may also be substituted, adding chopped green pepper.

Ed Stalcup

Breads

"I'm a wife of one of the firefighters you so graciously took care of. I could never thank you all enough for the love and kindness you showed to my husband and all the guys and gals who fought this terrible fire. It helps to know that a boyfriend or husband is being taken care of, when you, his wife or girlfriend, cannot be there.

In this terrible disaster, much good can be found in a stranger's kindness. God bless you all. Good luck in rebuilding the area."

Mrs. Chris Tallman
Fire Station # 76
San Bernardino County, Central Valley District
Fontana, CA 92335

COOGIE'S BEACH CAFE PUMPKIN BREAD

3 eggs
I cup vegetable oil
I cup sugar
2 1/2 cups chopped fresh
    pumpkin or I 3/4 cups
    canned pumpkin
3 cups unbleached flour
I teaspoon baking soda
I teaspoon salt
1/2 teaspoon nutmeg
I teaspoon cinnamon
I tablespoon vanilla
1/2 cup chopped pecans

Put the eggs, oil, sugar, and pumpkin in a blender. Blend well and put aside.

Sift flour, baking soda, salt, nutmeg, and cinnamon together in a bowl. Add the pumpkin mixture to the dry mixture; add the nuts. Blend well.

Pour into two 9" X 5" X 3" greased loaf pans. Bake I hour at 350°. Allow to cool 10 minutes in pan. Remove from pan and allow to cool completely.

Richard Tramonti
Coogie's Beach Cafe/Malibu

BEST EVER BANANA MUFFINS

4 bananas
1/4 cup sugar
I egg

I cup flour
1/2 cup oats
I teaspoon baking powder
I teaspoon baking soda
1/2 teaspoon salt
1/2 cup melted margarine
Optional: raisins, dates, walnuts

Blend the first three ingredients in a food processor. Mix the flour, oats, baking powder, baking soda and salt. Add the banana mixture and stir. Add desired optional ingredients.

Bake in muffin tins at 375° for 25 minutes. Makes 12 muffins

Chanchil Sundher

 This page sponsored by Coogie's Beach Café

KUGELHOPF

In a small bowl, dissolve yeast in water, add cooled milk and stir until blended. In a large bowl of electric mixer, cream butter and sugar until light. Add the eggs, one at a time, beating after each. Add the yeast mixture and beat until well blended. Sift flour again with salt into mixing bowl. Beat at medium to low speed until batter is smooth. Stir in the raisins, almonds, and lemon peel. Add chocolate chips if desired.

Butter a large Kugelhopf (10 cup) mold and sprinkle with the minced nuts, turning pan so the bottom and sides will be covered.

For an airy, coarse-textured coffee cake, turn the batter immediately into the buttered mold, and let rise as directed below. For a fine-textured coffee bread, cover bowl lightly and let rise in a warm place until doubled, about 2 hours. Beat batter down and turn into the buttered mold to rise.

Let rise in warm place until batter comes to about 1/4 inch of the top of the mold. If you use the traditional Kugelhopf mold or another 10-cup mold with tube, bake in a moderately hot oven (375°) for 50 to 60 minutes. If you use a 10-cup tubeless mold, bake at 350° for 65 to 70 minutes. Bake until cake tester comes out clean. Let cool in pan; turn out. Serves 12.

Toni Littlejohn

1 package dry yeast
1/4 cup warm lukewarm water
3/4 cup milk, scalded and cooled
   to lukewarm
3/4 cup butter or margarine
1/2 cup sugar
4 eggs, at room temperature
4 cups sifted flour
1 teaspoon salt
1 cup golden raisins
1/2 cup slivered almonds
1 tablespoon grated lemon peel
1/2 cup finely minced almonds

12-ounce package chocolate
   chips (optional)

DATE NUT LOAF

1 cup dates, quartered
1 cup water
1 teaspoon baking soda
3 tablespoons butter
3/4 cup sugar
1 egg, well-beaten
1 1/2 cups flour
1 teaspoon baking powder
3/4 cups chopped walnuts

Boil dates 3 minutes in water. Cool, then add baking soda. Cream butter, sugar and egg. Add date mixture and beat well. Then add flour, baking powder and walnuts. Pour into loaf pan. Bake in a moderate oven (about 350°) for 40 to 50 minutes.

Marilyn Reynold

ONION SHORTCAKE

1 large Spanish onion, sliced
1/4 cup butter
1 8-ounce package corn muffin
   mix
1 egg
1/3 cup milk
1 can creamed corn
2 drops Tabasco® sauce
1 cup sour cream
1 cup sharp Cheddar cheese
1/4 teaspoon dried dill weed
1/4 teaspoon salt

Sauté onion in butter and set aside. Mix together corn muffin mix, egg, milk, corn, and Tabasco® sauce.

Place in greased 8 inch square pan. Add the sour cream, 1/2 of the cheese, dill, and salt to the sauteed onions. Spread mixture carefully over the batter. Top with the remaining cheese.

Bake in a 425° oven for 30 minutes. Serve warm with dinner.

Louise Logan

MARMALADE CAFÉ'S OAT CURRANT SCONES

1 pound, 6 ounces all purpose
   flour
7 ounces rolled oats
5 ounces sugar
2 tablespoons baking powder
1 tablespoon salt
8 ounces butter
2/3 cup cream
4 eggs
1 tablespoon vanilla
6 ounces currants
4 ounces walnuts

Combine all dry ingredients with butter. Mix well. Add all wet ingredients.

Turn dough onto floured surface and gently pat into a circle 1-inch thick. Using a floured biscuit cutter, cut out scones and place on an ungreased cookie sheet 1 inch apart.

Bake at 375° for 20-30 minutes. Makes 24 scones

Stacey Aaronson
Marmalade
Malibu & Santa Monica

This page sponsored by Shelly Roman,
dedicated to Phil, Morgan, & Brittney

GRANDMA'S CHINA

It is early morning as I quietly open the screen door to my grandma's trailer behind our tiny farmhouse. I am overwhelmed by the smell of fresh bread and cinnamon rolls Grandma has been baking since before sunrise and I hear the percolator brewing what is, I'm sure, her second pot of coffee. She is sitting at the kitchen table refilling her tiny coffee cup. It is the same cup she was drinking her (shhhh) whiskey in all night. The same cup her mother drank her coffee from when my grandma was a little girl.

It was a Limoges cup from Havilland, France, my grandma told me for the 300th time, part of the set her mother got for a wedding present from her mother. It was the only thing my grandmother remembered about her mother. Her mother and father had been killed in a car accident when she was six. I often wondered why she didn't use a bigger cup since she would fill it up a dozen times before her percolator was empty. But she drank her coffee and her (shhh) whiskey out of this cup in memory of her mother she would say. It was her last memory of her and she feared losing even that if she drank from anything else. Then, HONK, HONK, the school bus is here and I run out the door letting the screen door slam, all the time thinking she would always be there to tell me stories.

After my grandmother's stroke left her mentally and physically incapable of taking care of herself, my father and I went to pack up her belongings. We found a neatly packaged box labeled for me. Inside was the set of china except for one cup, the cup she used every day. I found the cup tucked away in the back of her cupboard and inside it a note, "remember me".

At 11 a.m. on November 2, 1993, my next door neighbor called me at work and strongly advised me to come home now. He said a fire had started over the hill and might be coming our way. I left work and hurried to the Pacific Coast Highway only to be met by the worst traffic I had ever seen, with hundreds of fire trucks barreling north up the center divider. As I sat in traffic, I listened to the fire's progress on the radio and mentally did inventories of what I could grab if I had 30 minutes, 15 minutes, 5 minutes, etc...

It was 5 p.m. the next day before I could get to where our house used to be. It was getting dark, but it was easy to see that nothing was left. As I walked around the base of the foundation kicking up ash and broken pieces of charred glass and tile, I found one thing inexplicably unbroken. It was a tiny soot-stained cup. I will always remember you, Grandma.

-- *Rex Carey Arrasmith*

GRANDMA'S SODA BREAD

Smear 2 tablespoons butter in a 10" cast-iron skillet. Melt 2 more tablespoons butter in a separate pan and set aside. Preheat oven to 350o. Sift dry ingredients, add currants and toss to coat. Whisk the buttermilk, eggs, and the melted butter. Add to dry ingredients, and mix until just blended. Do not overmix. Spoon batter into prepared skillet, smooth top, dot with remaining 2 tablespoons butter. Bake until golden brown and puffed--about 1 hour.

Mike "Mack" McElvaney
Firefighter/Paramedic, Engine Co. 4, B Platoon

6 tablespoons butter
3 cups flour
1 1/2 teaspoons salt
1 tablespoon baking powder
1 tablespoon baking soda
3/4 cup sugar
1 1/2 cup currants
1 3/4 cup buttermilk
2 eggs, well beaten

NO FAT APPLE BREAD

Preheat oven to 350°. Spray 9 inch loaf pan lightly with PAM® to prevent sticking.

Mix all ingredients together very well (about 5 minutes). Bake 30 minutes or until golden brown. Cool five minutes then remove from pan.

Mix cream cheese icing ingredients together well with hand beater until smooth. Spread on top of cool bread.

Shelly Roman

1/2 cup Egg Beaters® (for 2 eggs)
2 cups grated apples
3/4 cup brown sugar
2 teaspoons pumpkin or
    apple pie spice
2 cups all purpose flour
1/4 cup non-fat plain yogurt
1/2 cup applesauce or 1/2 cup oil
1 1/2 teaspoons baking powder
1 teaspoon baking soda
1/2 teaspoon salt
1 8-ounce package no fat cream
    cheese
1 box powdered sugar
2 tablespoons vanilla
2 teaspoons grated lemon rind

47

MINCEMEAT MUFFINS

2 large eggs
3/4 cup vegetable oil
3/4 cup sugar
1/4 cup brown sugar or molasses
2 cups milk
1 1/4 cups mincemeat
1 1/4 cups Kellogg's All Bran or
    Natural Bran
2 1/4 cups all-purpose flour
2 teaspoons baking soda
2 teaspoons baking powder
1 teaspoon salt

Beat the eggs together with the oil in a large bowl. Beat in the sugars. Stir in the milk and mincemeat. Add bran and let stand for ten minutes.

Combine the flour, baking soda, baking powder and salt. Stir in the bran mixture until well mixed.

Fill greased muffin pan. Bake 375° for 18 to 20 minutes. Makes about 2 dozen muffins.

Batter will keep up to 3 weeks in the refrigerator. Stir batter mixture well before using.

Ann Stalcup

"The other day I astonished the line of people in the Malibu Post Office when I picked up my mail and yelled ecstatically, 'I've got two rejected manuscripts!' Having lost all of my records, I had no idea how many of my stories were sitting on editors' desks and how many were sitting at home. Now I have two more stories than I did on the day of the fire...

I pray that the earthquake victims have been as fortunate as I have and that all of them have had at least one angel who has done something special for them. I had so many angels. A hug, a smile, a touch on the arm, flowers from a garden--each can mean as much as more material gifts. Each will be accepted with a smile or tears, and each will help a friend or stranger become whole again."
-- *Ann Stalcup*

YORKSHIRE PUDDING

Yorkshire pudding is an English pudding usually served with roast beef. Yorkshire pudding may be baked like popovers, in small, heavy, pre-heated pans. But more frequently it is cooked in a shallow baking pan into which three or four tablespoons of the drippings from the roasting beef have been poured. In the old days, when meat was roasted in front of the fire, the baking pudding was placed under the roast for the last few minutes of cooking, so that it might absorb the last rich drippings or essence from the beef. It is served cut into squares and either placed around the roast or on a separate dish.

"Savory pudding" is a variation in which a little coarsely grated onion and a sprinkling of sage is added. A handful of plump seedless raisins may also be stirred into the batter just before baking.

Sift the flour and salt and mix to a batter with the unbeaten eggs and milk. Make the mixture smooth and creamy. If made an hour or more before baking, the pudding will be lighter than if prepared at the last moment.

In shallow pan put beef drippings; place the pan into the oven until sizzling hot. Place the batter in the hot pan and bake about 45 minutes with the oven at 450° the first 15 minutes and reduced to 375° for the remainder of the time.

I cup sifted flour
1/2 teaspoon salt
2 eggs
I cup milk
roast beef drippings

Honey Coatsworth

RED PEPPER CHEESE BREAD

1 large red bell pepper
1 package dry yeast
1 1/2 cup lukewarm water
1 teaspoon light brown sugar
2 teaspoons salt
1/8 teaspoon cayenne pepper
1 teaspoon dried hot red peppers
1 teaspoon sesame seeds
1 1/2 teaspoon dill weed
1/2 cup lukewarm milk
1 1/2 cup stone-ground whole
   wheat flour
1 cup grated Monterey Jack
   cheese
3 1/2 cups all purpose flour
1 tablespoon butter, melted

Roast bell pepper over gas flame, turning until charred. Wrap in a paper towel and place in a plastic bag. Cool, then remove skin from pepper, core, remove seeds and chop fine.

Place yeast in large bowl and sprinkle 1/4 cup water over. Let stand a few minutes, then stir in sugar, salt, cayenne, dried red peppers, sesame seeds, dill weed, milk, and chopped red bell pepper. Stir in whole wheat flour, alternating with remaining 1 cup water. Beat in grated cheese.

Slowly beat in 2 cups all purpose flour with a heavy wooden spoon. Transfer dough to floured bread board. Knead for 15 minutes, incorporating remaining 1 cup all purpose flour. When dough becomes elastic, let stand 5 minutes.

Divide dough in half. Roll into loaves and place in French bread pans. Cover bread pans with flour-rubbed tea towel and let stand 1 1/2 to 2 hours for bread to rise.

Preheat oven to 400°. Slash top of each loaf lengthwise with a sharp knife. Brush tops with melted butter. Place a roasting pan half filled with water in the bottom of the oven. Place the bread in the top third of the oven and bake 12 minutes. Reduce heat to 325° and continue baking 35 minutes longer. Cool on racks. Makes two loaves.

Melinda Littlejohn

SOFT PRETZEL ROLLS OR BAGELS

Soften yeast in 1/4 cup warm water. Add sugar, 1/2 cup flour, olive oil and salt to remaining water, then add the yeast and stir to blend. Add 2 1/2 cups of flour to yeast mixture to make a smooth dough.

Knead dough with remaining flour. Place dough in large mixing bowl and cover with plastic wrap. Let dough rise by 1/2. Remove and knead again on a lightly floured surface. Pinch off pieces of dough and roll between the palms of your hands to form a 6" by 3/4" long rope. Cross the ends and pinch the ends firmly to form a pretzel shape, or shape into a circle for bagels. Let dough rest for 30 minutes on parchment paper or a non-stick surface.

While forming the pretzels or bagels from the dough, bring a large pot of water to boil. Add 1 tablespoon sugar to the water. Drop the pretzels or bagels, one at a time, into the boiling water. Cook 1 minute and turn over and cook 1 minute more.

Remove with a slotted spoon and place on waxed paper. Brush with beaten egg and sprinkle with salt. Bake in a pre-heated 450° oven on a pizza stone (or cookie sheet lined with parchment paper sprinkled lightly with cornmeal) for about 10 minutes or until brown. Remove to racks.   Makes 15-20 pretzels or bagels.

Let's Get Cookin'
Westlake Village

3 1/2 to 4 cups flour
1/2 tablespoon sea salt
1 tablespoon sugar & 1 tablespoon
    for the boiling water
1 package dry yeast
1 cup warm water
1 tablespoon olive oil
kosher salt or coarse salt
2 egg yolks or 1 whole egg,
    lightly beaten

Pasta & Rice

"Now that we have returned to our own city, my crew and I have had time to reflect on the kindness offered to us by residents of the Cold Canyon Road area, in which my engine company was operating.

Our strike team of five engines was deployed on the fire for five straight days and the opening of your homes for telephone, bathroom, and shower use was of great help in maintaining my crew's readiness and morale. The food, candy, coffee, posters, and words of encouragement reminded us that we were helping protect a community that cares. These gestures were very refreshing, as often firefighters are unwelcome or attacked while trying to save lives and property.

The fire itself will not soon be forgotten, but I believe that the thing that will stand out in my memories most are the acts of appreciation and kindness from the residents of Calabasas and Malibu. Thank you."

John C. Lansing
Captain E-322A
Strike Team 6243A
City of Adelanto, CA 92301

BEAU RIVAGE RESTAURANT'S GNOCCHI ROMANA

Place the milk in a large saucepan and bring it to a boil over low heat. Add the first 1/3 cup of butter, cayenne pepper, nutmeg, and salt.

While stirring constantly, slowly sprinkle in the semolina. Continue to stir the mixture for 5 to 7 minutes more, or until it is of a smooth consistency.

Add the whipped egg yolks and stir them in so that they are well incorporated.

Add the first 1/3 cup of Parmesan cheese and mix it in well.

Pour the mixture into a greased baking dish (it should be 1" thick). Smooth it out with a spatula. Cover the dish and allow the gnocchi to cool.

Preheat the oven to 350°. Cut the gnocchi into squares or rounds. Place them in a buttered pan, brush on second 1/3 cup butter and sprinkle with the 1/4 cup Parmesan cheese. Bake for 7 to 10 minutes, or until they are lightly browned.

Beau Rivage Restaurant
Malibu

1 quart milk
1/3 cup butter
1 pinch cayenne pepper
1/8 teaspoon nutmeg
1 pinch salt
10 ounces semolina flour
8 egg yolks, whipped
1/3 cup Parmesan cheese, freshly grated

1/3 cup butter, melted
1/4 cup Parmesan cheese, freshly grated

 This page sponsored by Diane Randall

TROUT RAVIOLI

Filling:

3 to 4 tablespoons butter
2 medium whole trout, split open
    (about 1 pound)
1/2 cup dry white wine
juice of one lemon
1 tablespoon minced fresh Italian
    parsley
3 to 4 tablespoons heavy cream
salt and pepper to taste

Melt the butter in a large heavy skillet over medium heat. Reduce the heat to medium low and add the trout, skin side down and cook for about 5 minutes. Turn the trout over and cook until done—about 3 or 4 more minutes. Remove from the pan. Using a sharp knife, remove the skin from the fish. Carefully lift off the center bone, removing any tiny bones you see with tweezers. Cut trout into chunks. Pour wine into skillet and place over medium-high heat and cook until wine is reduced to 1 tablespoon. Stir in the lemon juice, and reduce once again to 1 tablespoon. Add the parsley and the cream, blending well. Add salt and pepper to taste. Stir in the trout. Blend with your fingers, feeling carefully for any bones. If you find any bones, remove them. Transfer the mixture to a food processor and mix using the pulse button, just until trout is chopped. Do not over process! You want texture. The mixture should be dry. If you put a spoonful in the palm of your hand and press down, there should not be any leaking moisture. If there is too much moisture, you will have soggy ravioli. Pour filling into a bowl and refrigerate at least 1 hour to firm up before making ravioli.

Mix flour and salt in food processor with a metal blade, until combined. Add eggs and pulse. As dough begins to form, add water only if dough is too dry. Dough should form a ball. Knead for about 30 seconds. Wrap ball in plastic wrap and allow to rest for 10 minutes to allow the glutens to develop.

Put pasta machine rollers on their widest setting. Feed the dough through. Fold the dough in half to make a square, and feed through the machine again. Repeat this folding and rolling about 7 or 8 times until the dough is smooth and elastic. Always make sure the dough is floured so as not to stick in the machine. Continue to roll the dough by lowering the rollers on the machine, one notch each time. Do not fold the pasta now, but rather keep rolling it and elongating it. Continue decreasing the spacing on your rollers until the thinnest setting. The pasta should be almost translucent. Cut the sheet in half, and lay half out on your worktable.

Place filling a tablespoonful at a time on the sheet of pasta, spacing each spoonful by about 1 1/2 inches. Continue until the sheet is filled. Brush the edges of the pasta with water, and lay the second sheet of pasta over, pressing down the sides. Cut raviolis with a pastry cutter, round muffin cutter or a round cutter with a scalloped edge. Place ravioli on a flour-dusted cookie sheet until ready to cook.

Blend the dill with the olive oil in a food processor or blender.

Cook ravioli in salted boiling water until the ravioli rise to the surface. Remove. Serve with warmed olive oil, dill, and garnish with dill oil. Serves 6

Gina Burrell

Pasta dough:

1 cup unbleached all purpose
    flour
1/2 cup semolina flour
1/2 teaspoon salt
2 large eggs
1 tablespoon warm water

Dill oil:

1 tightly packed cup of fresh dill,
    rinsed and dried
3 ounces extra virgin olive oil

LINGUINI PRIMAVERA

olive oil
3 cloves garlic, pressed
1 medium onion, peeled and
    chopped
1 package ground turkey

1 28-ounce can cut tomatoes
1 15-ounce can crushed tomatoes
3 carrots, peeled & diced

3 zucchini, diced
1/2 cup fresh basil, leaves only
1/2 cup fresh oregano, leaves
    only
fresh grated Parmesan or
    Romano cheese to taste
crushed red pepper flakes to
    taste

1 to 2 pounds linguini, cooked
    al dente

In a sturdy pan, sauté the garlic and onion until wilted, then add the turkey. Continue sautéing until the turkey is cooked through.

Add the tomatoes and carrots and simmer for about 7 minutes. Add the zucchini and simmer 5 minutes more. Add the basil and oregano and cook lightly until wilted.

Serve over the cooked linguini, sprinkled with cheese and red pepper flakes to taste.

Manuel R. Ramirez
Fire Station 88, Malibu

PESTO PIAMONTESA

In a blender, blend the basil leaves (no stems), parsley and olive oil until chopped. Add garlic and blend until the mixture becomes paste. Add grated Parmesan cheese and blend. Add butter and blend until pesto has a smooth consistency. Add additional olive oil as needed to blend into a smooth paste.

Hydrate the dried tomatoes and set aside to add to pesto when serving.

Cook the pasta al dente and top with the pesto, the dried tomatoes and pine nuts as desired. Serve with the salad and bread of your choice.

Robert Fidani
Fire Station 88, Malibu

2 packages fresh basil (about 2
  cups loose)
1 bunch parsley
1/3 cup olive oil
1/2 large head garlic
1 cup Parmesan cheese, grated
1/4 stick butter

1 package sun dried tomatoes
  (not packed in oil)
1 small package pine nuts

1 pound pasta (linguini or
  spaghetti)

RICE CASSEROLE

Bake all ingredients in 375° oven for about 40 minutes. This tastes even better reheated. For a crispy top, put the casserole under the broiler for a few minutes. Options you might add: 2 or 3 sliced mushrooms, leftover meat or chicken, frozen vegetables, and/or top with olive or tomato slices.

Fini Littlejohn

1 cup brown rice
2 cups water or broth
1 cup diced celery
1 cup diced bell pepper
1 10-ounce package frozen corn
1/3 cup wheat germ
1/2 cup chopped parsley
1/2 cup chopped water chestnuts
2 small cans or 1 large can
  tomato sauce

57

PENNE PUTANESCA

Penne are the hollow-tubed pastas cut on the bias. As a result, they resemble the tip of a quill "pen", hence the name.

"Putanesca" refers to a Southern Italian spicy red sauce with olives and capers, and means, literally, in the manner of the city streetwalkers. There are two theories regarding the origin of this nomenclature, one of which offers that it was something the ladies could prepare in between entertaining clients. Another, more obscure, theory suggests that it was something that the local chefs would prepare in exchange for services rendered. Either way, it is a light, yet surprisingly satisfying dish. It can be either a main course for a simple supper or, in smaller portions of course, an appetizer course of a larger meal. Because the penne has a "forgiveness" (unlike most pastas, it can sit for a short time without turning into paste), it can also be used in a small buffet.

And, for something completely different, try serving it cold as a refreshing summer luncheon dish. To do this you'll need to modify the taste and texture by adding a touch more salt and a little more liquid (tomato juice is an excellent way of thinning out the cold sauce).

On a final note: I find that not only is the cooking process more enjoyable but the final product is actually improved by playing Italian opera in the background while cooking this dish. (Pavarotti in Rigoletto, for example, brings out the lustiness of the flavors.)

Sauté the garlic slowly in the olive oil until it just starts to turn light brown. Quickly add the chili flakes and chopped anchovies. Pour in the wine and allow its alcohol to burn off for a minute. Then add the tomatoes, tomato paste, basil, and capers. Bring to heat and simmer for 15 minutes.

Add the olives and simmer for another five minutes. Put aside and cook the penne. The penne can be cooked for about ten or eleven minutes when you're ready to serve.

Or you can parboil the pasta in advance for seven minutes, stop its cooking by immersing in icy water for one minute and then draining completely and tossing with a little olive oil. Then, when you're ready to serve, simply lower the pasta into boiling water for 30 seconds or so to heat it. Then drain completely (do not rinse) and toss with the sauce. This is a fail-safe way of ensuring perfectly cooked pasta when you're dealing with the myriad details of entertaining friends for dinner.

Janet MacPherson

4 cloves garlic, sliced thin
1/3 cup olive oil
1/2 to 1 teaspoon dry crushed
    chili peppers, to taste
5 anchovies, chopped
1/4 cup white wine
1 1/2 pounds chopped tomatoes *
1 tablespoon tomato paste
8 basil leaves, julienned
3 tablespoons capers
1/3 pound Kalamata or Gaeta
    olives, pitted and quartered

salt and pepper to taste

1 pound dry penne (Di Ceccho
    brand preferred)

* If using fresh tomatoes, peel them. If using canned, buy San Marzano, an Italian designation of exceptionally rich tasting tomatoes.

LEMON-CHIVE LINGUINI WITH SMOKED SALMON AND GOLDEN CAVIAR

Pasta dough:*

(makes one pound)
1 cup unbleached all-purpose
    flour
1/2 cup semolina flour
1/2 teaspoon salt
2 large eggs
grated peel of one lemon
1/2 bunch chives, chopped

*Note: Packaged linguini may be substituted.

Mix dry ingredients in bowl of food processor fitted with metal blade. Add eggs, lemon peel and chives. If dough does not come to a ball, add warm water as needed, one tablespoon at a time. Run in processor to knead for about 30 seconds. Remove dough from processor, flatten out and wrap in plastic wrap and let it rest for 10 minutes to let the glutens develop.

Cut the dough in fourths, keeping unused portions wrapped in plastic wrap.

Set your pasta machine with the rollers at the widest setting. Feed the first quarter of dough through the rollers, and as it comes out, fold dough into thirds and repeat feeding the dough through the rollers. Repeat this process until the dough feels smooth. Always make sure to keep dough floured, so as not to stick in the rollers.

Set your rollers to the next closest setting and feed dough through. From this point on, there is no need to fold the dough. Simply roll through and with each successive closer setting of the machine, the pasta dough will get longer and thinner. Cut the dough in half so it is easier to handle. Take the machine to the second to last setting and roll the pasta dough twice through that setting. The dough should be somewhat translucent. Making sure the sheet is in a workable length, lay out to rest for about 5 minutes before cutting. Repeat with the remaining dough.

Place a linguini cutter on the machine, and begin to cut the pasta sheets. Place cut pasta on drying rack, or coil pasta into rounds. Repeat process with remaining dough. Let pasta rest for about 20 minutes before cooking. Pasta can be made earlier in the day and allow to dry before cooking.

Prepare the sauce: Heat butter in skillet over medium heat. Add shallots and saute until softened. Add the wine and reduce by 1/2 over medium high heat. Add the cream, white pepper and salt and bring to a boil. Reduce over high heat for about 3 minutes and remove from heat.

Bring a large pot of salted water to boil over high heat. Cook the pasta al dente, stirring with a fork to separate the strands. (Fresh pasta cooks in a very short time—much more quickly than dried.)

Drain the pasta. Toss with the hot cream and the smoked salmon, and heat the mixture through. Stir in the golden caviar, and taste for seasonings.

Serve on plates, garnished with a light sprinkling of chives and a small dollop of sevruga caviar. Serves 6.

Gina Burrell

Sauce:

2 tablespoons unsalted sweet
    butter
2 tablespoons minced shallots
1/4 cup dry white wine
1 cup heavy cream
freshly ground white pepper
salt to taste
6 ounces smoked salmon, cut
    into julienne strips
4 ounces golden caviar

Garnish:

2 ounces sevruga caviar
chopped chives

This page sponsored by Renny & Bernie Shapiro

61

The Firestorm Bomberos

Firestorm Fried Rice comes from the first-ever cooking lesson held at the Malibu Community Labor Exchange on the morning of November 2nd. My idea was to share an easy recipe with the men— basic Chinese fried rice. I brought a wok, portable burner, and the ingredients.

Halfway through the lesson, several men walked off to gaze skyward at the monstrous black plume of smoke blowing toward the ocean from the southeast. It wasn't until I got home that reality set in. The sheriff pounded on the door telling me to evacuate, the utilities went down one after another, and I was no longer in touch with the outside world or my family.

Villa Costera is a double dead-end street with eight houses and one exit road—Rambla Pacifico. Visitors were unlikely—as unlikely as the nine volunteer firemen from the Labor Exchange center who now stood at my back door. They were all smiling. They had been told to evacuate and were on their way to Los Angeles in the center van. But when they saw flames leaping behind our neighborhood, they agreed that I would need help.

My husband, Tom, arrived, having circumvented the gridlock on the Pacific Coast Highway by jogging from Sunset Blvd. in his business suit and the sports shoes he carries in his gym bag. He, two neighbors, and the men from the center started fighting the fire by defending the houses that were backed up to Rambla Pacifico. Flames hopscotched toward our enclave.

The men worked furiously, using rakes, shovels, damp rags and buckets of water to fight the blaze while I packed up our things and prepared to leave. Our access road was burning on both sides. It was so dark I turned on my headlights, but could see nothing but smoke and flames.

Later I learned that some of the men from the center stayed all night and assisted in putting out numerous small fires that continued to swirl into life. The fire trucks had gone many hours earlier. The men used chainsaws, shovels, and machetes to cut down burning branches. Villa Costera lost no structures but our storage shed.

Two weekends later, we hosted a pot luck for the Labor Exchange "Bomberos." And in the coming months the homeowners on upper Villa Costera would donate funds to purchase a trailer office for the Labor Exchange center to commemorate the bravery of the volunteer firemen that fateful day.

Mona Loo
Malibu Community Labor Exchange

FIRESTORM CHINESE FRIED RICE

Saute meat. Drain fat if using bacon. Use a small amount of vegetable or peanut oil if using ham or making this without meat.

Add cooked rice and stir fry until rice is dry and separated.

Add green onions and continue to stir fry.

When rice is very dry and well-fried, carefully add the beaten egg on the sides on the pan, or scoop a hole in the middle of the rice, so the egg can be on the actual metal to fry. If needed, you can add a small spoonful of vegetable oil directly to the side of the metal where you will begin frying the eggs.

Keep stirring the egg and rice mixture so the egg gets completely cooked. Add the vegetables. Stir fry 2 minutes more.

Season to taste. Serve immediately, or cover loosely until you are ready to serve.

Mona Loo

1/2 pound bacon or 2 slices of
  ham, chopped
4 cups cooked long grain white
  rice
1/2 to 1 bunch green onions
6 beaten eggs
1 box frozen green peas,
  thawed to room temperature
  and drained
salt and pepper and soy sauce
  to taste
Optional: any other vegetables,
  mushrooms or tasty leftovers
  you might have in your
  refrigerator

 This page sponsored by Marshall Ezralow

PIZZA WITH RATATOUILLE OF VEGETABLES AND PESTO

Pizza dough:
(Makes enough for 4 crusts)

I envelope active dry yeast
I 1/4 cups warm water
I teaspoon sugar
pinch salt
2 tablespoons olive oil
4 cups sifted all-purpose
    unbleached flour
corn flour

Ratatouille:

I green zucchini, sliced 2 1/2"
    long, 1/4" thick
I yellow squash, sliced 2 1/2"
    long, 1/4" thick
I large eggplant, peeled and
    sliced 2 1/2" long, 1/4" thick
I yellow pepper, julienned
I red pepper, julienned
I large onion, sliced thin
3 cloves garlic, minced
salt to taste
4 basil leaves, julienned
1/4 cup extra virgin olive oil

To make the pizza dough, dissolve yeast in 1/4 cup warm water. Set aside for 5 minutes. Dissolve the sugar and salt in the remaining water. Stir in the yeast and oil into the sugar and salt mixture, stir in remaining flour until a stiff dough is formed. Turn dough out onto a floured board and knead a few minutes. Place in a clean bowl and cover with plastic wrap. Allow to rise 1 hour.

Mix together zucchini, squash, and eggplant for the ratatouille. Sprinkle with salt and let stand thirty minutes. Pour out water and squeeze dry with paper towels.

Heat olive oil in pan. Sauté eggplant, zucchini, and squash until glden brown. Remove to plate. Add onions and peppers to pan. Sauté until lightly golden. Add garlic. Sauté a few minutes more. Remove from heat. Stir in basil. This may be prepared a few days before. Cover and refrigerate.

To make the pesto, combine all ingredients except oil and cheese in the bowl of a food processor. Process, slowly adding the oil. Remove to a bowl and mix in the Parmesan cheese.

Shown in the photo top left is "Penne Putanesca", at right
is "Trout Ravioli" with dill oil, and in front, "Lemon-Chive
Linguini with Smoked Salmon and Golden Caviar".

When dough is ready, divide into 4 equal parts. Use one part and freeze remaining dough not being used that day. Roll the dough into a 12" circle. Place on a pizza pan that has been lightly oiled and sprinkled with corn flour. Spread on the pesto. Alternate cheeses over pesto. Top with ratatouille. Bake at 500° on lowest shelf for 5 to 7 minutes or until bottom crust is brown. Then place under the broiler for 2 minutes and serve.

Cathy Rogers

Pesto:
1 cup fresh basil
1/4 teaspoon salt
freshly ground pepper
3 cloves garlic
2 tablespoons walnuts
1/2 cup extra virgin olive oil
1/2 cup freshly grated Parmesan
    cheese

Cheese:
1/4 pound Mozzarella, sliced thin
1/4 pound Munster, sliced thin
1/4 pound Jack, sliced thin
1/4 pound Fontina or Jarlsberg
    Swiss, sliced thin

MONROE'S RESTAURANT RIGATONI DUDLEY'S

In a large skillet, heat the heavy cream, and then add egg yolk, pepper, butter and cheese. Heat until mixture starts to thicken. Add sausage and noodles to the sauce and heat for 3 minutes. Add the broccoli and serve.

Monroe's Restaurant
Malibu

8 ounces heavy cream
1 egg yolk
1 teaspoon black pepper
1 tablespoon butter
4 heaping teaspoons Parmesan cheese, freshly grated
1 sweet Italian sausage, sauteed in a pan with the casing removed
8 ounces rigatoni noodles, cooked al dente and drained
10 broccoli florets, cooked

65

PASTA CON SALSICCIA

While struggling to drive home to Malibu on one of those pea-soupy nights in 1954, I was close to panic. Nothing looked familiar. How could it look familiar? I was in Inglewood. No help coming from the snoring dog beside me. She was used to my navigation dyslexia.

When the fog lifted, I spotted bright neons and drove to an Italian restaurant. This was the beginning of my gastronomical love affair.

I decided that I had to have the recipe and thus began a week of batting my baby greens, sweet-talking (begging?) in my kitchen Italian...and pouting. It was demeaning and I decided to give it up when this gorgeous Latin flashed his pearly whites and with Oxford English said, "Would you honor me by accepting my recipe of Pasta Con Salsiccia?

2 pounds ground chuck
2 cups diced onions
2 cloves garlic
2 pounds hot Italian sausages
   (optional)
3 6-ounce cans tomato paste
2 1/2 cups cooked or canned
   plum tomatoes
I sprig each fresh rosemary,
   basil, and oregano
I pinch of anise
I cup dry red wine

I pound pasta of your choice

In a huge pot, brown the ground chuck, diced onions, garlic, and Italian sausage in a small amount of oil.

After the meat is seared, reduce heat and add all the other ingredients. Simmer for 3 hours over low heat.

Cook the pasta al dente. Serve with a green salad and garlic bread. Oh, yeah, pick up a jug of Chianti, yes? ECCELENTE APPETITO!

Jini Dill

66

DRAGO RISTORANTE'S MACCHERONCINI AGLI SCAMPE E TARTUFO NERO

MACCHERONCINI WITH LANGOSTINO AND BLACK TRUFFLES

Remove the shells from the langostino; set the meat aside. In a saucepan, add olive oil and when warm, add the shells from the langostino and saute for about 3 minutes. Add the vegetables and the thyme and parsley. Saute for 8 minutes. Add the cognac and wine, let evaporate, then cover the ingredients with water and add the tomato. Cook over low heat until liquid reduces by half. Pour the liquid through a sieve, pressing on the shells to get any extra liquid.

In another saucepan, place the liquid and the truffles, whipping cream, salt, and white pepper. Reduce until you have a creamy texture.

In a saute pan, add one tablespoon of butter and the langostino meat. Saute and set aside.

Cook the maccheroncini in boiling salted water until al dente, drain, and toss with the sauce. Place pasta on a serving plate and garnish with the reserved langostino meat. Serve hot. Serves 4

Drago Ristorante
Santa Monica

1 pound maccheroncini pasta
4 tablespoons olive oil
20 medium langostino
1 teaspoon onion, chopped
1 teaspoon carrot, chopped
1 teaspoon celery, chopped
1 small bunch fresh thyme
1 small bunch fresh Italian
  parsley
3 ounces cognac
1 cup white wine
1 cup fresh tomato, chopped

2 teaspoons black truffles,
  julienned
1 cup whipping cream
white pepper to taste
butter

67

Main Courses

A RECIPE FOR FISH BAKED IN ASHES:

No cheese, no nonsense! Just place it tenderly in fig leaves and tie them on top with a string; then push it under hot ashes, bethinking thee wisely of the time when it is done, and burn it not up.

> *Archestratus*
> *Gastrology, 4th Century B.C.*

"One of the many helpful things—from hugs to housing—our friends and family shared with us after we lost our Rambla Pacifico home of 20 years was recipes we had previously shared with them. It seems that special family recipes should have a place on an evacuation list right up there with family photo albums, art work and address books."

Ron and Sally Munro

68

BOUILLABAISSE CARDINALE ITALIANO

Sauté the onion, garlic, parsley, celery, and green pepper in the olive oil over a medium-high flame until they are golden brown. Add the seasonings and all other ingredients except the seafood. Reduce the heat and cook very slowly for 1 1/4 more hours.

After the sauce has cooked and has been seasoned to taste, add all the seafood and cook for 15 to 20 minutes, gently stirring occasionally.

Serve steaming hot in large soup bowls with plenty of crusty sour dough or French bread and a good Chardonnay. Bon Appetit!

Tony Cardinale
Seafood Manager, Hughes Market
Malibu

1/2 cup olive oil
1 onion, chopped
5 cloves garlic, chopped
1/4 cup parsley, chopped
2 stalks celery, chopped
1 small bell pepper, seeded, cored, and chopped

1 tablespoon each salt, dried basil and paprika
1/2 cup sherry
1 cup dry white wine
2 cups solid pack tomatoes with juice
2 bay leaves
1 cup water
1 cup tomato sauce
1 cup fresh Roma tomatoes, chopped

1 large Dungeness crab, cleaned and cracked
1/2 pound large scallops
1 pound large shrimp, cleaned and deveined
3/4 pound petite lobster tails, split
1 1/2 pounds little neck clams
3/4 pound eastern mussels
1 pound firm fresh fish such as halibut, sea bass or albacore, cut into bite-sized pieces

 This page sponsored by Arnold & Karen York

69

PRIMI RESTAURANT'S INVOLTINI DI SWORDFISH AND SHRIMP

3 shallots, chopped
1 cup vermouth
1 tablespoon green pepper

4 ounces sweet butter
12 medium shrimp, cleaned
1 bunch thyme, chopped
juice of 1 lemon

9 ounce piece of swordfish

1 tomato, chopped
1 head raddicchio

Chop two of the shallots and add to a sauté pan. Add the vermouth and pepper, and allow to simmer for 3 minutes on low heat.

Add the butter a little at a time and mix with a whisk until the mixture becomes creamy.

Slice the swordfish into thin slices and roll around the shrimp. Marinate for 1/2 hour in a bowl with the last chopped shallot, lemon juice, thyme, and a pinch of salt.

Cook on a griddle for 3 minutes.

Quickly fry raddicchio and serve it as a bed on each plate under the shrimp.

Serve with the butter sauce and the chopped tomato on top.

Serves 4

Primi Ristorante
West Los Angeles

This page sponsored by Elliot Handler

SALMON NARANJADO

In a blender, mix the juice of the orange and lime and the other flavoring ingredients until well blended.

In a baking dish, arrange the fish and baste with the juice mixture. Marinate for 1/2 hour refrigerated. Remove from refrigerator and baste again.

Bake at 325° for approximately 15-20 minutes or until white gel surfaces from fish. Do not overcook.

Serve with Mahatma Ready Wild Rice Mix, cooked as directed, and steamed vegetables.

1 orange
1 lime
1 clove elephant garlic
1 teaspoon fresh ginger
1 teaspoon lemon pepper
1/2 teaspoon orange rind peel
1/2 teaspoon lime rind peel
1/2 teaspoon salt
1/3 cup olive oil

2 pounds salmon fillets

Manuel R. Ramirez
Fire Station 88, Malibu

This page sponsored by Marca Helfrich

BIBI'S SUN-DRIED TOMATO SAUCE

1 ounce (2/3 cup) sun-dried
    tomatoes* (Do not use
    oil-packed)
2 tablespoons catsup
2 tablespoons tomato paste
2 tablespoons balsamic vinegar
2 tablespoons fresh lemon juice
2 tablespoons cider vinegar
1/4 cup vegetable oil
1 tablespoon fresh tarragon,
    chopped fine
1 tablespoon fresh chives,
    chopped fine
1 teaspoon capers, chopped fine
1/2 teaspoon fresh garlic,
    chopped fine
1/2 teaspoon fresh ground black
    pepper

    *Sun-dried tomatoes can be
made easily at home. Just cut 14
ripe Roma tomatoes in half and
place, cut side up, on a parchment-lined cookie sheet. Sprinkle
with sea salt. Place in the oven at
the lowest temperature (130°
overnight). Take them out in the
morning. Store in the refrigerator.

This favorite recipe of ours was lost in the fire, which also ate our computer. Fortunately, I'd given the recipe to a new Malibu friend as we passed out leaflets in front of Hughes Market last fall just before a much more eventful election day than any of us had bargained for! (The day of the fire.)

The original recipe is from the Accomac Inn in Pennsylvania, but I adapted it for easier preparation. It tastes best if made ahead of time and will keep in the refrigerator for a week. It is delicious as a sauce for cold, poached salmon or on any grilled fish steaks such as shark or swordfish. It can also be stirred into mayonnaise for an interesting vegetable sauce.

Simmer the sun-dried tomatoes in a cup of water for about 3 minutes and cool in the water. Chop up the other ingredients while you wait for the tomatoes to hydrate and become cool enough to handle. Drain the simmer liquid into a glass or ceramic bowl. Chop the tomatoes as fine as possible. Combine the tomatoes and all other ingredients, plus 1/2 cup of water, in the bowl with the reserved liquid and mix well. Allow to stand, covered, at least two hours, or overnight.

To use as a marinade for fish, take 1/2 the mix, adding 1/2 cup of water and marinate fish in a glass container, covered and chilled, for 2 hours. Brush on marinade while grilling and serve the reserved sauce with the fish on the side.

John and Bibiana Mays

GULF SHRIMP WITH POBLANO BUTTER

Combine the Poblano butter ingredients. Thread the shrimp on skewers and grill over hot coals or a gas grill, basting with the Poblano butter. Serve over rice with a dab of the remaining butter on top.

Note: The Poblano butter may be doubled and any left over can be frozen for use later with grilled fish or chicken.

Walt Shirk
Captain/Paramedic Engine Co. 1, B Platoon
Santa Monica

16 Gulf shrimp (colossal size)
    peeled and deveined

Poblano butter:

1/4 pound unsalted butter,
    softened
1 1/4 Poblano peppers, roasted,
    seeded and finely diced
1 tablespoon minced cilantro
1 tablespoon minced garlic
salt and pepper to taste

TUNA BURGER

Place tuna in bowl of Cuisinart® and process with steel blade. Add minced scallions, soy sauce, Tabasco® sauce, and salt and pepper to taste. Pulse a few times to mix. Form into four patties.

Heat oil in a non-stick skillet until smoking. Sauté patties for 30 seconds on each side. Spread brioche toasts with mayonnaise and top with tuna burger. Add garnish as desired.

Gina Burrell

1/2 pound fresh Ahi tuna
2 teaspoons soy sauce
8 drops Tabasco® sauce
4 tablespoons extra virgin
    olive oil
2 scallions, minced fine
salt and pepper to taste
8 slices round brioche bread,
    toasted
4 tablespoons mayonnaise

BUBBA'S "Just Like My Momma Used To Make" SHRIMP

For the "shrimp boil":
1 onion, chopped
2 bay leaves
1 teaspoon black peppercorns
1 teaspoon white peppercorns
7 cloves garlic, mashed
2 stalks celery, leaves and all,
    chopped
1 tablespoon salt
splash of Tabasco Sauce
2 small lemons or 1 big one,
    thinly sliced
2 pounds fresh shrimp, washed

Shrimp sauce:
1 small onion, chopped
1/4 cup lemon juice
1/2 teaspoon Tabasco Sauce
1/3 cup prepared horseradish
1/4 cup chili sauce
1/4 cup salad oil
salt to taste

4 stalks celery, finely diced
1 or 2 green peppers, finely diced
1 bunch green, sliced
1/2 cup parsley, finely chopped

Put everything but the lemons and the shrimp in a big pot with about a half gallon of water and bring to a boil. Lower the heat and simmer for about 10 minutes. Add the lemons and the shrimp and simmer about 3 to 5 minutes. (This will all depend on the size of the shrimp, how good your stove is and what you consider "simmering".) You'll know if it's done, because they'll turn pinkish-red the way shrimp does, but don't cook it so long they start to curl up real tight, or they'll be tough and chewy.

Drain it all right away and stick it in a big bowl of ice water to cool it down fast. Then comes the only real hard part. Peel the shrimp and take out that little string of poop that runs along their back. Now they're ready for the next step.

Put the stuff for the sauce all in a blender and blast it to kingdom come. When it's all smooth, pour it into a nice big bowl and add the shrimp and cut vegetables.

Mix it all together and keep it in the icebox while you make the fried green tomatoes:

This is easy. Just cut the tomatoes in about half-inch slices, spread them out and sprinkle them with salt and pepper on both sides.

Heat about a half-inch of the oil in a large skillet. When it's pretty good and hot, pour the cornmeal onto a plate, dip the slices of tomato in it to get them all nicely coated and slip them into the skillet. You'll have to do a few at a time unless you have more than one skillet. When you figure they're done on one side, flip them over with a fork and brown the other side. Take them out and drain them on paper towels. Keep them hot in a low oven while you do the rest, but make it quick, so they don't get soggy.

Now you're ready to eat. Put about four fried tomatoes on each plate, then scoop out a nice big serving of the shrimp and put it right in the middle. You might want to sprinkle a little more chopped parsley on top to make it look pretty, and bring a bowl of lemon wedges to the table, but what you don't want to do is stand around and talk. Eat it while it's hot and cold!

This ought to take care of six people pretty well.

Alan Roettinger

6 green tomatoes
   (Don't pick them too green; they should be starting to turn yellow just a bit or they got no flavor.)
about a cup of cornmeal, but you may need more, so have it handy
salt and pepper
corn oil for frying

STEAMED SALMON WITH SPINACH LEAVES & ONION MUSHROOM CHILI RELLENOS

Tomatillo sauce:

1 tablespoon canola oil
1 onion, chopped
3 cloves garlic, minced
6 tomatillos, chopped
6 tomatoes, chopped
1 Anaheim chili, roasted and
    chopped
1 teaspoon cumin
1/2 teaspoon Hungarian paprika
sea salt
1 teaspoon sugar
1 1/2 cups chicken broth

Black bean sauce:

1/2 cup black beans, soaked
    overnight in cold water
1 onion, chopped
3 cloves garlic, minced
1 quart chicken broth or water
sea salt

For tomatillo sauce, heat 1 tablespoon canola oil, and in it saute onion until golden brown. Add garlic, tomatillos, tomatoes, chili, cumin, paprika, salt, sugar, and chicken broth. Simmer about 30 minutes. Strain, reserving liquid. Place in pan and reduce until lightly thickened. Reserve

For black bean sauce, drain soaking water from black beans, then cover them with chicken broth or fresh water in a 2 quart saucepan. Add onion and garlic. Season with sea salt. Bring to a boil, reduce heat and simmer 2 hours or until tender. Strain, reserving liquid. Place 3/4 beans (saving the remainder for garnish) and 1 cup of the reserved liquid in a food processor and process until smooth. Strain beans and add more chicken broth if too thick. Reserve.

Begin making chili rellenos by heating 2 tablespoons olive oil in a pan. Saute onions and mushrooms until golden brown. Reserve and cool. Mix mushrooms with shredded Jack cheese. Divide mushroom mixture into 6 portions. Shape with your hands into a chili shape. Place into roasted Anaheim chili. Beat egg whites and salt until light peaks form.

Gradually add flour. Heat canola oil to 375°. Place a little egg white mixture on a plate. Place one filled chili over egg white mixture on the plate and place more egg white mixture on top of chili. Spread with knife to enclose chili with egg white batter. Carefully push chili into hot oil, making sure egg white batter is all over chili. With spoon, spoon a little oil over top. Cook until golden and turn over. Remove and place on a paper towel. Continue with the remaining chiles and batter. Reserve oil, keeping it hot.

Carefully place spinach, one leaf at a time, into the hot oil. Cook 15 seconds on each side. Stand back from pan while spinach cooks, as it may splatter. Continue with remaining spinach. Place cooked pieces on a paper towel-lined cookie sheet. The spinach may be prepared earlier in the day.

Cut the salmon into 1/2" strips. Roll up into a medallion and tie with string to secure. You should have 18 medallions--three per person. Season with sea salt and freshly ground pepper and steam 5 to 8 minutes in a steamer.

Heat tomatillo and black bean sauces. Place chili in 375° oven for 15 minutes. Pour black bean sauce on each plate. Pour tomatillo sauce around black bean sauce. Scatter cooked whole black beans over. Place 1 chili on each plate. Spread mustard on bottom of salmon, and place 3 pieces of salmon on the other side of plate. Remove strings. Garnish salmon with spinach leaves. Serve and enjoy.

Cathy Rogers

This page sponsored by Cathy, Jeff, Ryan, and Chad Rogers

Chili rellenos:

2 tablespoons olive oil
1 onion or 2 shallots, chopped
6 shiitake mushrooms, diced
1 1/2 cups shredded Jack cheese
6 Anaheim chiles, roasted and peeled
6 egg whites
5 tablespoons flour
pinch sea salt
3 cups canola oil

Steamed salmon:

30 leaves spinach, cleaned and dried
1 1/2 pounds salmon, filleted and skinned
freshly ground pepper
sea salt
Dijon mustard

PONZU CHICKEN & STUFFED POTATOES

Ponzu chicken:

4 boneless skinless chicken
    breasts
8 cloves fresh garlic
1/2 cup flour
fresh tarragon
white wine
Ponzu (Japanese sauce available
    at health food stores)

Stuffed potatoes:

4 potatoes, scrubbed and poked
    with a fork
fat-free cheddar cheese
green onions
fat-free milk
paprika
vegetable salt

The morning I woke up to find ash covering the porch of my Point Dume home, it seemed the wise thing to evacuate to the Salvadorean-Central American Refuge Center in Hollywood where I had arranged to stay for the duration of the fire.

I stopped at a friend's house to let her know my plans. She informed me that she had four people staying with her whose homes had burned to the ground. I managed to drive to East Malibu, where I work as a gourmet chef, and get to my boss' home to rescue a meal I had made before the fire. I was able to share this meal with those fire victims. It included this chicken dish and these potatoes.

Cut the chicken into fingersize pieces. Roll in flour and snipped tarragon. Sauté the garlic in Ponzu sauce. When the sauce thickens, add a couple of tablespoons of wine. Cook chicken on each side for about 4 or 5 minutes.

Bake the potatoes at 350° for one hour. Slice them in half and scoop out the innards. Mash the potato and blend in the cheese and onions. Stuff the potato shells, and, if desired, sprinkle with paprika and vegetable salt. Reheat in the microwave for 1 minute or in a conventional oven for 10 minutes.

Valerie Sklarevsky

CHICKEN TANDOORI

This is an easy recipe, especially for large groups. It can be made the day before. And it requires no knives - just forks!

Saute the chicken in some canola oil with the garlic. When almost cooked, add the onions, peppers, and tomatoes. Remove from heat, add rice and spices. Bake in a 375° oven for approximately 30 minutes. When ready to serve, you may want to sprinkle crushed peanuts, yogurt and shredded coconut on the casserole. This is optional.

June Foray

2 cups diced raw chicken
2 cloves garlic, minced
1 cup diced onions
1 cup diced green peppers
2 diced tomatoes
1 cup hot cooked rice
1 teaspoon cinnamon
1 teaspoon turmeric
1 tablespoon cumin
salt according to taste

POLLO VERDE

Boil the chicken until cooked--about 15 minutes. Shred and set aside.

Boil tomatillos until cooked--about 7 to 10 minutes. Place in a blender and add the garlic, red pepper, and salt. Blend and add to chicken in a sauce pan. Simmer for about 10 minutes and serve hot with rice, beans, and corn tortillas. This is low-fat and low-cholesterol.

Manuel R. Ramirez
Fire Station 88, Malibu

3 half chicken breasts, skinless
      and boneless
2 pounds tomatillos
2 garlic cloves, pressed
crushed red pepper to taste
salt to taste

LULA'S CHICKEN STUFFED WITH DRIED RED CHILIS AND ORANGE MARINADE

10 chicken breast halves, boned, and skinned

1/2 cup olive oil
10 garlic cloves, left whole
1 cup white onion, sliced thin and julienned
12 dry red chilis (4 each Ancho, Pasilla and Guajillo), seeded, stemmed, and julienned with scissors
1 dry Chipotle chili, prepared as in the red chilis
2 cups fresh orange juice
10 whole berries allspice
2 inches Mexican canela (cinnamon stick)
2 bay leaves--crush when adding to marinade

sugar to taste
extra orange juice for sauce

Pound chicken breasts with a mallet and season with salt and pepper.

Make the marinade: Heat the 1/2 cup olive oil, and add the 10 garlic cloves and brown them. Remove them from the oil, reserving them for another use. Add the 1 cup julienned onion and sauté for a minute or two. Add the julienned chilis and stir to combine. Add the orange juice, allspice, cinnamon, and bay leaves. Bring to a boil. Season with salt and pepper, cook another minute to combine flavors. Remove from heat and let cool completely before adding to chicken.

Make the filling for the chicken: Heat the 4 tablespoons butter and the 2 tablespoons oil and saute the 1/4 cup chopped onions, and then add the mushrooms and saute. When they release liquids, saute another minute and season well with salt and pepper. Remove from heat and let cool completely before filling chicken.

Place an epazote leaf down the center of a chicken breast, fill with some of the mushroom mixture and tuck up the ends. Continue for the remaining leaves and breasts. Place the chicken in a glass baking dish.

Strain the cinnamon stick, bay leaf and allspice from the marinade and pour over the chicken to cover. Allow to marinate at least 4 hours. The flavor is best if allowed to marinate overnight.

Shown in the photo top left is "Corn Diego", at right is "Fish a la Lulu" with fried spinach leaves, and in front, "Lemon Basil Grilled Chicken" with garlic mashed potatoes and potato chip.

Bake the chicken, covered, at 400° for 30 minutes. Make a sauce by taking 1/2 the marinade from the cooked chicken and blend with a little sugar and some orange juice to get a sauce consistency.

Serve the chicken sliced with sauce, white rice, and black beans. Serves 10

Gerri Gilliland
Inspired by Lula Beltran/ Lula Restaurant
Santa Monica

Filling:
4 tablespoons butter
2 tablespoons vegetable oil
1/4 cup chopped white onion
1 1/2 pound white mushrooms, chopped
1 1/2 pound fresh shiitake mushrooms, stemmed & chopped
10 leaves fresh epazote (available in Mexican markets--if unavailable, omit)

LEMON BASIL GRILLED CHICKEN

Combine first 6 ingredients in a shallow baking dish. Add the chicken, turning to coat both sides.

Refrigerate for one hour to marinate.

Take chicken out of pan and grill or broil.

Estelle Grundstein

1/2 cup olive oil
1/4 cup lemon juice
2 tablespoons white wine vinegar
1 teaspoon grated lemon peel
1 tablespoon dry basil
2 cloves garlic, minced

6 boneless, skinless chicken breast halves

ALICE'S RESTAURANT STIR FRIED SEA SCALLOPS

1 cup salted Chinese black beans, soaked overnight and rinsed
1 tablespoon ginger, minced
1 tablespoon garlic, minced
1/2 teaspoon chili flakes
1/4 cup oil

1/4 cup sherry wine
1/4 cup soy sauce
1 cup water
1 1/2 tablespoon sugar
2/3 cup oyster sauce
2 tablespoons cornstarch

5-6 ounces cooked angel hair pasta
1 red pepper, julienned
1 yellow or green pepper, julienned
1/4 cup scallions, chopped

6 ounces bay scallops

Place beans, garlic, ginger, and chili flakes in a food processor. Process until coarsely chopped.

Combine sherry, soy sauce, water, sugar, oyster sauce, and cornstarch together in a mixing bowl and whisk until well blended.

Heat oil in a frying pan until smoking and then add bean mixture and cook for 3 minutes. Add sauce mixture and simmer on medium to low heat until thick. Allow to cool, then refrigerate until needed.

Sauté angel hair pasta in a small amount of oil in frying pan to a light brown color. Remove from pan to warm platter.

Sauté peppers and scallions 2-4 minutes. Add bay scallops and sauté an additional 2-3 minutes. Add prepared black bean sauce and cook until hot.

Pour over sautéd angel hair pasta and serve.

Alice's Restaurant
Malibu

 This page sponsored by Anita Green

FISH A LA LULU

Rub the fish with minced garlic and allow it to absorb the flavor for a few hours in the refrigerator.

Cut the tomatoes in 1/4 inch dice and place in a colander for 1/2 to 1 hour to drain excess juice. Toss in the minced garlic and shallots. Add basil, lemon juice, salt and pepper, olive oil and capers.

Quickly sear the fish on an oiled griddle, and finish cooking to your taste in a 350° oven. Do not overcook.

Serve on individual plates with the tomato coulis under the fish. Serves four.

Lou Siemons

1 to 1 1/2 pounds fresh halibut
    fillet or salmon fillet, skin
    and bones removed
minced garlic

Tomato coulis:
7 fresh ripe Roma tomatoes
1 tablespoon minced garlic
2 tablespoon minced shallots
1/2 cup fresh basil leaves,
    chopped coarsely
1 teaspoon fresh lemon juice
salt & ground pepper to taste
1 tablespoon olive oil
1 tablespoon drained capers

This page sponsored by Mary Lou & Jerry Siemons

MALIBU SEAFOOD CEVICHE

1 1/2 pounds bay or calico
    scallops
3 medium tomatoes, peeled,
    seeded and chopped
1 minced jalapeño chile
1/3 cup olive oil
ground pepper to taste
1 medium onion, peeled, sliced
    and chopped
1/4 cup chopped cilantro

2 large limes
3 avocados, peeled and sliced
1 small cucumber, diced

Place scallops in a medium glass bowl. Cover shellfish with the lime juice. Cover bowl and refrigerate until the shellfish loses its transparency and becomes opaque. This takes about 24 hours.

Drain juice from shellfish. Combine them with the tomatoes, chiles, olive oil, pepper, onion, and cilantro. Squeeze juice from the two limes over mixture and toss well.

Arrange sliced avocado on top, sprinkle with diced cucumber and serve.

Serves 6 to 8.

Malibu Seafood
Malibu

 This page sponsored by the Malibu Rotary Club

GIDGET'S TURKEY MEAT LOAF

Mix all ingredients well.

Form into a loaf and bake uncovered at 350° to 400° for one hour.

Sprinkle a little paprika on top before serving.   Salt and pepper to taste. HANG TEN!

Gidget Zuckerman

1 pound ground turkey meat
1/2 cup sauerkraut
1 egg
3 tablespoons bread crumbs or matzo meal or cornflake crumbs
1/2 teaspoon poultry seasoning
2 tablespoons sour cream or yogurt, plain or non-fat
1 teaspoon brown sugar
1 teaspoon prepared mustard
1 to 2 teaspoons catsup
dash of salt and pepper

BURRITOPITAS TIROPITAS

Mix the eggs, Feta and cottage cheese together with a fork. Melt butter in a small saucepan. Butter each side of the tortillas. Pour 1 tablespoon of the egg/cheese mixture into the center and roll up like a tube.

Butter a shallow baking pan and place the tiropitas side-by-side in the pan and brush the tops with butter. Bake at 350° about 30 to 35 minutes. May be served whole or cut in half.

4 eggs
1/2 pound Feta cheese
1/2 pound butter
2 tablespoons cottage cheese
1 dozen flour tortillas

Dorothy Wilson

BABY BEAUJOLAIS

In my lingering life I've been booed and hissed,
I'm always in love—but seldom get kissed,
I've stuck my chin out and been smacked by a fist,
But there's no great vintage wine I've ever missed
or a baby Beaujolais!

Whenever I bet on the horses, they always stumble in last,
The girls I adore have a dubious past,
My choices in life would make you aghast,
But in choosing a wine, my nose is unsurpassed
or a baby Beaujolais!

The vintage years, the vintage years
The ones I've chosen have dried my tears,
Have quenched the fire of my fears,
I bet I'll live a million years!

When all the stock markets crash, ripping my lifestyle apart,
When my wives all split and my friends depart,
And I sit around waiting for World War III to start,
A great vintage wine will comfort my heart--
or a baby Beaujolais!

Yes, a great wine is the state of the art,
or a nubile Beaujolais!

Burgess Meredith

SADDLE PEAK LODGE RESTAURANT
QUAILS WITH RED WINE SAUCE

Salt and pepper the quails and saute them until lightly brown in two ounces of the butter until fully cooked. Remove and keep warm. Degrease the pan and add the demi-glace with the Beaujolais and shallots. Add the coriander and let it simmer. Crush the garlic and add it to the sauce. Place the quails in the sauce for about one minute.

To serve, place each quail on a crouton. Finish the sauce by adding the remaining one ounce of butter and pour it through a fine strainer over the quails. Top with lightly sauteed julienned ham.

2 semi-boned quails
salt and pepper to taste
3 ounces butter
2 ounces demi-glace
1/4 cup Beaujolais (or other red wine)
1 teaspoon chopped shallots
1 pinch ground coriander
1 whole, unpeeled garlic clove
2 toasted croutons
1 ounce julienned smoked ham

During the devastating fires in our neighborhood last fall, we were able to help our neighbors with their horses and gather them into our parking lot. When the fires were finally put out, we had a thank-you picnic for the firefighters to show our appreciation and gratefulness for the safety of the valley.

Saddle Peak Lodge Restaurant
Calabasas

 This page sponsored by W.I. Simonson

TURKEY WITH OYSTER STUFFING

Oyster stuffing:

1 cup butter
2 large onions, finely chopped
1 1/2 cups green celery leaves,
    finely chopped
2 tablespoons each parsley and
    green pepper, chopped
salt to taste
1/2 teaspoon each black pepper,
    thyme, mace, cloves
1 teaspoon sage
3 quarts soft bread crumbs
2 pints drained, chopped oysters
    (preferably from the
    Northwest)

This is my favorite recipe for turkey. It's an old recipe that was given to me by a dear friend. It was on my computer, which I managed to save from the fire.

I publish many journals for nurses. One of my editors is head of the nursing education and research department at NPI/UCLA, and she too loves to cook. Knowing I had lost all my cookbooks, she worked with the office of the Dean of UCLA School of Nursing and organized a "help our colleague rebuild her life" cookbook collection. Liz made sure I had an historical collection, too--with at least one book from several "eras" of cooking. Now I have a wonderful collection of cookbooks...and I love it!

Melt the butter, then stir in the onions, celery leaves, and all other spices and herbs. Cook 3 to 4 minutes over low heat, stirring almost constantly. Add bread crumbs; mix thoroughly. Last of all, add the oysters. Voila!

Turkey preparation: Wash cavities with cold, running water. After draining, drying, and sprinkling the inside of the turkey with salt and pepper and desired seasonings, stuff it lightly with the oyster dressing.

Rub the bird lightly with bacon drippings, sprinkle with salt and pepper. Place breast side down in pan; lay 2 slices of salt pork over it and begin roasting at 450° for 15 to 20 minutes to sear.

Reduce heat to 350° and add gravy seasonings to pan.

Pour 2 cups of water into the pan. Cover the bird with cheesecloth (and foil if necessary). Baste frequently.

Bake until internal temperature (of bird, not the stuffing) is 185°. Do not overcook. Enjoy that luscious gravy.

Margo Neal

Gravy seasonings:

turkey & bacon drippings
salt park
1 large onion, chopped
1 stalk of celery, scraped
    and chopped
2 medium carrots, scraped
    and chopped
2 bay leaves
12 sprigs parsley
3 sprigs celery leaves
2 sprigs of fresh thyme
    (or 1/2 teaspoon dried)
2 whole cloves

This page sponsored by Carole, Martin, David, & Adam Hamburger

HONEYMOONER'S CHILI

6 tablespoons butter or
    margarine
2/3 pound chuck steak, coarsely
    ground
2/3 pound chuck steak, cubed
    into quarter pieces
1 green pepper, seeded, cored
    and chopped
1 large onion, chopped
1 clove garlic, minced
3 tablespoons parsley, chopped
2 tablespoons chili powder
2 teaspoons salt
1/2 teaspoon black pepper
1/4 teaspoon coriander
1/2 teaspoon cumin
1 16-ounce can tomatoes,
    including liquid
4 dashes Tabasco® sauce

In a 4-quart casserole, melt 3 tablespoons of the butter or margarine in the microwave on High for 45 seconds. Pierce cubed steak with a fork and add it. Microwave on Medium High for 5 minutes. Pour off 3 tablespoons of the liquid.

In a 2-quart casserole, place the ground meat in chunks. Microwave on High for 3 minutes. Drain off all liquid. Add this meat to the cubed meat casserole.

In the same 2-quart casserole, combine the green pepper, onion, garlic, and parsley with 3 tablespoons of butter or margarine. Cover with plastic wrap and microwave on High for 5 minutes.

Add the vegetables to the 4-quart meat casserole. Stir in the chili powder, salt, pepper, coriander and cumin. Add the tomatoes and hot sauce.

Cover casserole with plastic wrap. Microwave on High for 10 minutes. Let stand, covered, 10 minutes before serving.

Beverly Taki

90

BAMBU RESTAURANT'S MARINATED GRILLED LAMB CHOPS

Whisk all ingredients together and chill overnight in the refrigerator to blend flavors.

Add lamb to marinade and allow to sit for 1 hour.

Grill lamb or saute in a hot pan 3 to 4 minutes per side.

Bambu Restaurant
Malibu

2 cups oil (1 cup each canola
    and olive oils)
1/4 cup Worcestershire sauce
1/4 cup balsamic vinegar
4 cloves garlic, crushed
1 bunch rosemary, chopped
1 teaspoon each salt and pepper

16 French lamb chops

Dear Bambu,

Our department has a long and proud history of sending mutual aid assistance to other communities in need. Although our firefighters sometime actually compete for the opportunity to serve on a strike-team, there is a price to pay. We leave our worried families and the comforts of home behind for several days at a time. We work long hours and catch what sleep we can lying on the ground dreaming of hot showers. By opening your restaurant to us, you not only provided hundreds of firefighters with an excellent hot meal, you also promoted some healthy interaction between them by serving as a social center. The open, friendly nature of your staff further motivated this extended "family" feeling. The gratitude extended by you and the whole Malibu community was overwhelming and certainly appreciated by all the firefighters. Our best wishes to you all for a quick and complete recovery.

Thomas D. Cole
Strike Team XBU3001
Paradise Fire Department
Paradise, CA 95969

JAMBALAYA

5 basil leaves, minced
2 teaspoons fresh oregano,
    minced
1 teaspoon fresh thyme, minced
1 teaspoon sea salt
1 teaspoon cayenne pepper
1/4 teaspoon red pepper flakes
1/2 teaspoon freshly ground
    pepper

3 tablespoons olive oil
1/2 cup Black Forest or other
    smoked ham, cubed
2 large smoked sausages*, or
    1 cup broken bulk sausage,
    cooked and chopped
1 large onion, chopped
1 cup celery, chopped
1/2 cup each red and yellow
    bell pepper, chopped
1 chicken breast, uncooked, cut
    into bite-size pieces
5 cloves fresh garlic, minced
8 Roma tomatoes, peeled and
    chopped

*See optional recipe for Spicy
Turkey Sausage

An Englishman travelling through Louisiana in the early 1800's stopped in quite late at the New Orleans Inn. He requested room and dinner. The proprietor, having very little left for dinner, said to his cook, Jean: "Jean, Balayez" (which means "blend good things together"). The guest was very pleased and bragged about having eaten Jean Balayez. This term has since been transformed into JAMBALAYA!

Combine the first 7 ingredients in a bowl. Reserve.

Preheat oven to 350°. Heat the olive oil in a 12" ovenproof skillet. Add the ham and smoked sausage and cook until crisp, about 5 minutes, stirring frequently. Mix in onion, celery, and yellow and red pepper and cook until crisp-tender, about 5 minutes, scraping the bottom of the pan occasionally. Add the chicken, increase the heat to high, and cook 1 minute, stirring. Reduce the heat and add garlic and reserved seasoning mixture. Stir a few minutes to blend the flavors. Add the tomatoes and cook a few minutes more.

Pour in tomato sauce and simmer 5 minutes. Add the broth and bring to a boil. Remove 1 cup of the broth. Stir in the green onion and mix in the orzo. (You may wish to grill the shrimp separately and add it to the dish at the very end. If not, add it to the jambalaya 5 minutes before the orzo is finished.) Cover and bake in oven 25 to 30 minutes.

Reduce broth you removed from jambalaya by 1/2, swirl in optional 3 tablespoons butter to make sauce.

For individual serving presentations, place an empty 3" tuna can ring in center of plate. Put jambalaya in and pack down. Remove ring. Arrange shrimp (if not already cooked in the orzo mixture) around jambalaya or plate. Put a little sauce on each shrimp. Serve with potato chips.

Serves 12

Louis (Ed) Hill

1 cup tomato sauce
2 cups chicken broth
1 cup orzo pasta
1/2 cup chopped green onion
24 medium raw shrimp, shelled and deveined.
If desired, marinate shrimp in 1 tablespoon olive oil, 1/2 teaspoon crushed red pepper and 2 tablespoon chopped chives
3 tablespoons butter (optional)

Spicy Turkey Sausage:*

3 pounds ground turkey thigh
2 teaspoons sea salt
1/4 cup minced herbs
5 garlic cloves, minced
1 teaspoon paprika
1/2 teaspoon red chili flakes
1/4 cup corn syrup
1/4 cup honey
1/4 cup dry mustard

Mix ingredients and let marinate two days. Place in sausage casing and smoke. Freeze until needed.

 This page sponsored by Louis & Lyllis Hill

93

TRA DI NOI RISTORANTE OSSOBUCO ALLE VERDURE

2 medium-sized zucchini,
ends trimmed
2 medium-sized carrots, scraped
1 medium-sized red onion, peeled
1 medium-sized celery stalk
20 sprigs Italian parsley,
leaves only
6 ossobucho (veal shank cut into
1 1/2 inch slices, with bone
and marrow)
1/2 cup unbleached all-purpose
flour
6 tablespoons (3 ounces) sweet
butter
2 tablespoons olive oil
2 tablespoons tomato paste
1/4 cup lukewarm homemade
chicken or beef broth
2 cups dry white wine
salt and freshly ground black
pepper
1 teaspoon dried thyme

Cut the zucchini, carrots, onions, and celery into small pieces and put them in a bowl of cold water along with the parsley. Let soak until needed.

Tie each ossobuco all around the sides with string. Lightly flour the ossobucho on both sides but not on the edges. Heat the butter and oil in a casserole over medium heat and, when the butter is completely melted, add the meat and saute until it is golden brown on both sides (about 3 minutes on each side).

Meanwhile, dissolve the tomato paste in the broth, then add it to the casserole and cook for 2 minutes. Add 1/2 cup of the wine to the casserole and let it evaporate for 10 minutes.

Drain the cut up vegetables and add them to the casserole. Cover and cook over medium heat for 20 minutes. Taste for salt and pepper. Turn the ossobucho over and add the remaining wine and the thyme. Cover the casserole again and cook for at least 35 minutes longer.

Meanwhile, prepare the vegetables. Fill 4 bowls with cold water. Put the peas in one and let them soak for 1/2 hour. As each of the other vegetables is cleaned, put it in its bowl to soak for the same length of time. Clean the string beans, removing the ends and string. Scrape the carrots and cut them into quarters lengthwise. Then cut each quarter into 2-inch pieces. Remove the strings from the celery and cut each stalk into three long strips. Then cut each strip into 2-inch pieces.

Bring 4 small pots of cold water to boil, then add coarse-grained salt. Place each vegetable in its own pot and boil them until each is cooked but still firm, about 15 minutes. Drain the vegetables and let stand until needed.

When the meat is tender, taste for salt and pepper and transfer the meat to a serving platter. Cover to keep ossobucho warm.

Pass the remaining contents of the casserole through a food mill, using the disc with the small holes, into a large bowl. Return the passed ingredients to the casserole and cook over medium heat for 15 minutes, or until a thick and smooth sauce is formed.

Meanwhile, heat the 6 tablespoons of butter and the oil in a saucepan. When the butter is completely melted, add the boiled vegetables and season them with salt, pepper, and nutmeg. Saute gently for 5 minutes.

Return the meat to the casserole with the reduced sauce to reheat and to absorb some of the sauce. Remove the strings from the ossibuchi and serve. Arrange each serving on a plate with an ossobuco, some of the sauce and some of the sauteed vegetables. Serves 6

Tra Di Noi Ristorante
Malibu

Vegetables:

3/4 pound fresh peas, shelled
3/4 pound string beans
3/4 pound carrots
3/4 pound celery hearts
coarse-grained (kosher) salt

6 tablespoons (3 ounces) sweet
    butter
2 tablespoons olive oil
salt and freshly ground black
    pepper

MEAT PIES (FATAYES)

Filling:

2 pounds coarsely chopped lamb
1 large onion, finely chopped
juice of 2 large lemons
2 tablespoons fresh or dried mint
salt and pepper to taste

Dough:

2 packages dry yeast
1/2 teaspoon sugar
1 3/4 cup warm water
5 cups flour
1/4 cup oil
1 teaspoon salt

This recipe is from my grandmother who was known for her many Middle Eastern dishes. Her cooking was so good, my uncles would fight over equal portions of her food. She lived 97 years and, as fate would have it, she died on November 2, 1993. My other losses were so great that day, I never really had time to mourn the loss of my grandmother. So, in her honor, I submit this recipe. Her whole family misses her and her cooking.

Mix all filling ingredients together well and allow to marinate overnight.

Dissolve the yeast with the sugar and warm water and set aside until foamy. Gradually combine the flour, oil, and salt with the yeast mixture. Knead until smooth. Adjust the dough with additional water or flour as needed. Make the dough into a large ball and put in a warm place to rise for about an hour.

Form balls the size of golf balls and again set aside to rise for an hour. To shape meat pies, roll out the balls of dough to about 5" (depending on desired size). Fill with meat mixture. Pinch up three corners tightly to form triangles.

Place pies on a lightly greased baking sheet and bake at 400° for 25 minutes. Serve hot.

DeDe, John, & Jeremy Gooden

 This page sponsored by Dede, John, & Jeremy Gooden

Shown in the photo top left is "Jambalaya" with potato chips, Bambu Restaurant's "Marinated Grilled Lamb Chops", and in front, Saddle Peak Lodge Restaurant's "Quails With Red Wine Sauce".

CHOUCROUTE

Sauté carrots, onions, and garlic in butter over medium heat until tender. Add to sauerkraut in a mixing bowl.

Parboil potatoes. Add to sauerkraut and vegetables.

Grill sausages, ham, and bacon. Drain off fat. Combine the meat with the sauerkraut and other ingredients. Stir in chicken broth and wine, mixing well.

Bake in a large covered casserole dish at 350° for 1 hour. Serves 6.

Ann Fulton

1 tablespoon butter
1/2 cup grated carrots (2 small)
1 cup chopped onions (2 medium)
3 cloves garlic, minced
1 1-pound jar sauerkraut, drained and rinsed

6 baby red potatoes

1 half ring smoked sausage, cut into 6 pieces
1 half ring Kielbasa sausage, cut into 6 pieces
6 breakfast sausage links
1 cup cubed ham steak
6 slices bacon, diced

1 cup chicken broth
1/2 cup dry white wine

Desserts

1 or 2 quarts of rum
1 cup butter
2 large eggs
1 cup dried fruit
1/2 cup mixed nuts
baking powder
1 teaspoon soda
1 tablespoon brown sugar
1 tablespoon lemon juice

*Editor's note: While we believe
that some may find this recipe
comforting should the sirens begin
to wail, we do not recommend
beginning this Firestorm Rum Cake
if evacuation may be necessary!

FIRESTORM RUM CAKE*

Before you start, sample the rum to check for quality.
Good, isn't it? Now, go ahead. Select a large mixing bowl,
measuring cup, etc.

Check the rum again. It must be just right. To be sure rum
is of highest quality, pour 1 level cup of rum into a glass and
drink it as fast as you can. Repeat if necessary.

With an electric mixer, beat 1 cup dried butter in a large
fluffy bowl. Add won jugger of thugar and beat again.
Meanwhile, make sure that the rum is of finest quality. Try
nother cup. Open shecond quart win necessary.

Now, add two arge leggs, too cups fried druit and beat till
high. If druit gets stuck in beaters, just pry it loose with a
drewscriber. Time to sample the rum again, shecking for
transcisticity. Next shift 3 cups of pepper or sale (it really
doesn't matter). Sample the rum again.

Nauw shift in 1/2 pint of jemon luice. Fold in chopped butter
and strained nuts. Add 1 lablespoon of brown thugar, or
whatever color you can find. Whip into shape. Grease
oven and turn cake pan to 20 gredees. Now, pour the
whole mess into coven. Sheck the rum again, if any, and
flop into bed.

Itsh bin a nice cake!

Louis E. Hill

CHOCOLATE TORTE

Melt the chocolate, and set aside to cool.

Cream the butter, gradually adding the sugar. Cream until light and fluffy. Add the melted chocolate, and then the egg yolks one at a time, beating well after each.

Beat egg whites until stiff.

Sift flour and baking powder. Fold into the batter.

Pour into 8" cake pan which was well buttered and bake at 325° to 350° for 1 hour.

For filling, cream the butter and sugar until light and fluffy. Gradually add melted chocolate and eggs.

When cake is cold, cut in half and fill with half the cream filling. Decorate the outside of the cake with the remainder of the cream filling.

Lisa Fuchs

6 ounces unsweetened baking chocolate
1 1/2 sticks sweet butter
1 1/4 cups sugar
8 large egg yolks
10 egg whites
1 cup cake flour
1 teaspoon baking powder

Cream filling:

1 1/2 sticks sweet butter
1 cup sugar
2 eggs
2 1/2 ounces unsweetened baking chocolate, melted

This page sponsored by Katherine Price

DELICIOUS FARM COUNTRY BAKED APPLES

6 very large Roman Beauty
    apples (Do not substitute
    any other variety)
fresh lemon juice
pure maple syrup
cinnamon
large walnut pieces

This simple but elegant recipe uses no fat and is low in calories. It comes from my family, who owned an apple farm back East. We are rebuilding in Malibu and hope to break ground this year. Can't wait to get back again!

Core apples almost to the bottom. Leave the bottom intact.

Arrange in a baking dish, cored side up. Fill 3/4 of the cored space with lemon juice. Add maple syrup to the top of the core. Sprinkle heavily with cinnamon and scatter walnut pieces over the tops.

Bake at 350° for 1 1/2 to 2 hours, until centers are soft and skin of apples pulls away. Watch that the juices coming from the apples do not burn away. Add some lemon juice to the pan if necessary.

Serve plain, with the juices from the pan, or with chunks of sharp cheddar cheese, or with scoops of Haagen-Dazs vanilla non-fat frozen yogurt.

Serves 6

Dorothy H. Kagon

TEXAS SHEET CAKE

In a saucepan, combine water, butter or margarine, shortening and cocoa. Cook and stir until boiling. Remove from the heat.

In a mixing bowl, combine the flour, sugar, baking powder, cinnamon, and salt. Add the hot cocoa mixture and mix until smooth. Add the 1/2 cup buttermilk, eggs and vanilla. Beat well.

Pour into a greased 15" X 10" X 1" baking pan and bake at 375° for 20 minutes or until it tests done in the center.

In a saucepan, combine the butter, buttermilk and cocoa powder for frosting. Cook, stirring, until boiling. Remove from heat. Blend in the rest of the ingredients and beat until smooth. Immediately pour frosting over warm cake.

Alice Joynt

1 cup water
1/2 cup butter or margarine
1/4 cup shortening
1/4 cup unsweetened cocoa
   powder

2 cups all-purpose flour
2 cups granulated sugar
1 teaspoon baking powder
1 teaspoon ground cinnamon
1/2 teaspoon salt
1/2 cup buttermilk
2 eggs
1 teaspoon vanilla

Frosting:

1/2 cup butter
6 tablespoons buttermilk
1/4 cup cocoa powder
1 16-ounce package powdered
   sugar, sifted
1 teaspoon vanilla

MRS. (DONNOVAN) FIELD'S COOKIES

This basic cookie recipe is for two batches of cookies. Extra dough freezes well in containers. Chocolate chips (chunks or morsels), raisins, soaked in orange juice or sour cream, coarsely chopped nuts, chopped fresh cherries, apricots, apples or blueberries may be added just before baking. Make a variety of cookies--be creative! Sprinkle powdered sugar on some and add large chunks of chocolate to the center of others.

5 sticks margarine ("I can't believe it's not butter"® or any low-fat, low cholesterol product)

1 cup brown sugar

3/4 cup maple sugar (or 1/2 maple and 1/4 date)

3/4 cup raw sugar or turbinado (if unavailable, use brown sugar)

2 large eggs

2 teaspoons fine quality vanilla

2 1/2 cups all-purpose flour

1 cup finely chopped nuts-- almonds, walnuts, macadamias, pecans, or a combination

2 teaspoons baking soda

1 1/2 teaspoons salt

2 teaspoons cinnamon

1 teaspoon nutmeg (freshly- ground if possible)

5 cups Quaker Oats® (old-fashioned uncooked)

2 teaspoons very finely chopped orange rind (no white)

Heat oven to 375°. Lightly spray cookie sheets with Pam® or similar product. Beat margarine with sugars until fluffy. Beat in eggs and vanilla.

Add combined flour, baking soda, salt and spices. Mix well. Add orange rind and finely chopped nuts. Stir in oats. Place any extra dough in freezer containers and store in freezer, then stir in chips, etc.

Drop by rounded tablespoonfuls onto cookie sheet and flatten with a fork. Bake about 9 minutes for soft cookies, more for crisp ones. Large cookies can be baked for as long as 15 minutes, but watch carefully after 10 minutes--they can brown quickly. Remove to wire racks and sprinkle with powdered sugar if desired. Cool.

Donnovan Field

SAINT HONORÉ DARK GANACHE COOKIES

To make ganache, place the chocolate in a bowl. Bring the cream to a simmer over medium-high heat and pour over the chocolate. Gently stir with a balloon whisk until smooth and shiny. Let cool to room temperature.

Beat the butter and powdered sugar until very pale. Add cocoa, 3 ounces of the ganache and the cream, mixing thoroughly. Slowly add the flour and egg white and mix thoroughly. Use a pastry bag fitted with a medium-large star tip to pipe 1 tablespoon each teardrops (or simply drop by tablespoonfuls) onto parchment-lined baking sheets. Bake at 375° for 12 to 15 minutes. When cool, use remaining ganache to sandwich them together, back to back.

Saint Honoré Bakery
Malibu

chocolate ganache:

6 ounces bittersweet chocolate,
    finely chopped
1/4 cup cream

cookies:
10 ounces butter
6 ounces powdered sugar
2 ounces powdered cocoa
6 ounces chocolate ganache
2 tablespoons whipping cream
11 ounces flour
1 egg white

1 box plain yellow cake mix
1 package instant vanilla pudding
4 eggs
1/2 cup water
1/2 cup oil
1 ounce Baker's® German sweet
    chocolate, grated
6 ounces semi-sweet chocolate
    chips
1 cup pecans, chopped
8 ounces sour cream
1 cup grated coconut

DR. RUTH'S "BETTER THAN SEX" CAKE

Mix all ingredients together and bake in a greased and floured Bundt pan for 55 minutes at 350°. Enjoy!

Ruth B. Rubinstein, Ph.D., MFCC

1 cup butter
3/4 cup white sugar
1/4 cup brown sugar, firmly
    packed
1 egg
1 teaspoon vanilla
1/4 cup molasses
1 cup flour, sifted
1 teaspoon baking soda
3 cups oatmeal
3 teaspoons cinnamon
1/2 7 ounce package coconut
sunflower seeds to taste
3 cups large chunks
    chocolate chips

DR. RUTH'S "TO LIVE FOR" OATMEAL CHOCOLATE CHIP COOKIES

Blend together butter, sugars, egg, vanilla and molasses. Add the rest of the ingredients. Mix well. Drop by teaspoonfuls onto cookie sheet.

Bake at 350° for 10 minutes.

Ruth B. Rubinstein, Ph.D., MFCC

 This page sponsored by Dr. Ruth Rubinstein

APPLE TORTE

In a food processor, put butter, 1/3 cup of sugar, and 1/4 teaspoon vanilla. Blend in flour, pulsing on and off; put in the bottom of a springform pan.

1/2 cup butter
1/3 cup sugar
1/4 teaspoon vanilla
1 cup flour

Filling:

In a separate bowl, add softened cream cheese and 1/4 cup of sugar. Mix well. Add the egg and 1/4 teaspoon vanilla. Mix well. Pour over dough bottom.

1 8-ounce package cream cheese
1/4 cup sugar
1 egg, beaten
1/4 teaspoon vanilla

In another bowl, add 1/3 cup of sugar, cinnamon & apples. Place in a circle on top of cream cheese mixture. Sprinkle with almonds.

1/3 cup sugar
1/2 teaspoon cinnamon
2 cups sliced, peeled McIntosh apples
1/4 cup sliced almonds

Bake at 450° for 10 minutes, then reduce the oven temperature to 400° and continue baking for 20 to 25 more minutes.

Loosen torte from the sides of the pan; take off the rim. Cool. Serve on a silver platter.

Margo Neal

105

14 eggs
2 cups sugar
10 tablespoons flour plus a bit
   more for dusting the pan
10 tablespoons plus 3/4 cup
   Dutch process cocoa

20 ounces bittersweet chocolate,
   finely chopped
8 ounces bittersweet chocolate
   shavings
5 teaspoons good quality instant
   coffee, dissolved in 4
   teaspoons hot water
1 teaspoon instant coffee, dry
the juice and finely grated zest of
   7 Valencia oranges
3/4 pound unsalted butter,
   softened, plus a bit more for
   buttering the baking pan
1 teaspoon cream of tartar
2 tablespoons superfine sugar
3/4 cup Grand Mariner liqueur
6 cups fresh raspberries
1/2 cup cream

THE CHOCOHOLIC'S NIGHTMARE
A Small Dessert Buffet by Alan Roettinger

This small but deadly spread should take care of even the hardest-core chocolate personalities. Sort of like a wine-tasting for chocophiles.

CHOCOLATE-ORANGE CAKE WITH RASPBERRIES

First, bake the cake: Whisk 6 of the eggs with 1 cup sugar over hot water until it is smooth and warm to the touch. Beat with an electric mixer until tripled in bulk. Sift together 10 tablespoons of flour and 10 tablespoons cocoa, then fold them into the egg mixture. Pour into a buttered and floured 9" springform pan and bake at 350° for about 25 minutes, or until done. Cool on a rack about 30 minutes, remove the ring and let cool completely. Slice into four layers. Remove the top 3 layers of cake from the pan, then close the springform around bottom layer. Combine 3/4 cup of the fresh orange juice and 1 cup Grand Marnier.

Melt the chopped chocolate in a bowl over hot water. Mix the coffee with 8 egg yolks and the orange zest. Stir 8 ounces soft butter into the chocolate then stir in the yolk mixture. Whip the 8 egg whites until foamy, then add the cream of tartar and beat to soft peaks. Add superfine sugar and continue beating until it is stiff, another minute or so. Fold the whites gently but thoroughly into the chocolate mixture and proceed immediately to assemble the cake.

Brush 1/4 of the juice/Marnier mixture onto the bottom cake layer. Spread one third of the mousse, then scatter 1 1/2 cups of the raspberries evenly over it. Top with another cake layer and repeat the process two more times, finishing with a layer of cake. Cover assembled cake with plastic wrap and then refrigerate at least 4 hours.

Combine 1 cup sugar, 3/4 cup cocoa, 1 teaspoon instant coffee powder and 1/2 cup cream in a saucepan and stir it to a thick paste. Place the pan over a medium-low heat and stir constantly until the sugar is all dissolved. Add 1/4 cup butter and cook until it is smooth and shiny, about 5 minutes or more. Let it cool slightly while you set up the cake.

Remove the cake from the springform pan and place on a serving plate. Working quickly, pour the melted cocoa mixture on top of the cake and spread all around with a long metal spatula. Before the coating is set, press chocolate curls gently into the sides of the cake, reserving about 1/2 cup.

Place the chocolate leaves on the cake in a random pattern. Sprinkle on the remaining 1/2 cup of chocolate curls, and place a few raspberries here and there. Cut the cake with a hot, dry knife and serve at room temperature with vanilla custard sauce on the side. (Recipe follows)

Alan Roettinger
The Sweet Life/Agoura

Chocolate leaves:

24 lemon leaves, washed & dried
(available at florist shops)
12 ounces bittersweet chocolate,
finely chopped

Melt chocolate in a stainless steel bowl over hot water. Coat the back sides of the lemon leaves with melted chocolate and set them on a baking sheet. Place in the freezer for about 5 minutes.

Peel the chocolate free from the leaves. Store the chocolate leaves in refrigerator until ready to finish and serve the cake.

MOCHA PROFITEROLES

3/4 cup unsalted butter plus a bit more for the baking sheets

1/4 teaspoon salt

I cup flour plus a bit more for dusting the baking sheets

4 eggs, plus I beaten egg for the wash

9 ounces top-quality milk chocolate, finely chopped

I 1/2 tablespoons instant coffee powder, dissolved in 1/4 cup hot water

I tablespoon Kahlua liqueur

2 1/2 cups heavy whipping cream

I teaspoon instant coffee powder, dry

I cup sugar

3/4 cup Dutch process cocoa

Bring I cup water and the salt to a boil with 1/4 cup butter, cut into pieces. Away from the heat, add a cup of flour all at once, stirring with a wooden spoon till well mixed. Return to heat and cook, stirring for about 5 minutes, till dough comes away from the sides of the pan. Remove to a clean bowl and let cool 5 minutes. Add 4 eggs, one at a time, mixing well.

Preheat the oven to 400°. Butter and flour two baking sheets. Using a pastry bag fitted with a medium plain round tip (about # 6 or 1/2 inch), pipe the dough in small I 1/2" balls onto the baking sheets. Brush them with the beaten egg wash and let them dry for 20 minutes before baking for 20 to 25 minutes until lightly browned. Turn off the oven, open the door a crack, and let them cool slowly for about an hour. Remove them from the oven and let them cool completely. Poke a small hole in the bottom of each pastry through which to pipe the filling.

In a metal bowl set over hot water, melt the milk chocolate with the dissolved coffee and Kahlua, stirring gently. Remove from the heat and let it cool till it no longer feels warm. Beat I 1/2 cups cream to soft peaks and gently fold in. Immediately scrape into a pastry bag fitted with a medium-small star tip and quickly pipe into the pastry shells. Keep the profiteroles chilled until ready to serve.

Combine the sugar, the dry coffee powder, the cocoa and the remaining cream in a heavy saucepan. Stir well and cook over medium heat until the cocoa melts and the sugar dissolves. Add the remaining butter and cook about 5 minutes more until smooth and shiny. Keep warm. To serve, place profiteroles on a platter and drizzle a little of the warm sauce over each one. Serve the remaining sauce on the side.

CHOCOLATE-ALMOND TART

Grind the almonds and sugar in a food processor until fairly fine. With the motor running, pour in the butter. Press the mixture into a 9" tart pan. Bake at 350° for about 20 minutes, or until lightly browned. Remove to a rack and cool. Place the bittersweet chocolate in a large bowl. Heat the cream until just beginning to simmer and pour it into the bowl. Stir very gently until smooth, add Amaretto and combine thoroughly. Pour all at once into the baked shell, shaking gently to distribute evenly. Using parchment cones or squeeze bottles, pipe little dots of white and milk chocolate on the surface of the tart, then draw a toothpick through each one to form little "hearts". Transfer to refrigerator and chill at least 4 hours. Cut with a hot, dry knife into thin wedges and serve at room temperature.

10 ounces toasted almonds
3/4 cup sugar
7 tablespoons bittersweet
    chocolate, finely chopped
1 3/4 cups cream
1/4 cup Amaretto
1 ounce milk chocolate, melted
1 ounce white chocolate, melted

Alan Roettinger
The Sweet Life/ Agoura

CHOCOLATE-MINT TRUFFLES

2 pounds bittersweet chocolate,
   finely chopped
1 1/2 cups cream
1/4 pound unsalted butter,
   softened
1/4 cup peppermint schnapps
about 1 cup of cocoa for dusting

Vanilla Custard Sauce:
(serve with Chocolate-Orange Cake)

8 egg yolks
1 cup sugar
pinch of salt
1 Tahitian vanilla bean, steeped
   for 10 minutes in 2 cups of
   whole milk or half-and-half
1/4 cup whipping cream, chilled

Beat yolks, sugar and salt until
very pale and thick. Stir in hot
milk. Cook over simmering water
until the custard thickens enough
to coat a spoon. Remove from
heat, stir in the cream and let cool,
stirring occasionally. Refrigerate
until ready to use.

Place 1 pound of the chocolate into a bowl. Heat the cream in a heavy saucepan until it just begins to boil. Pour it over the chocolate and let it sit a couple of minutes. Very gently stir the chocolate with a whisk until you get a dark, shiny, smooth mixture. Add the butter and stir it in. Add the schnapps and gently stir it in well. Cover the bowl with plastic wrap and refrigerate it about four hours, or until firm.

Once the truffle mixture is firm enough to handle, scoop out about two teaspoons at a time and form a rough ball with your fingertips. Then roll it between your palms to form a nice ball. Repeat with the remaining chocolate and freeze the balls on a baking sheet. Melt the remaining chocolate. Spread the cocoa around on a tray. Dip the frozen balls in the chocolate, letting the excess drip off, and then place them on the tray with the cocoa. Shake the tray to roll the balls around, coating them evenly. Store the truffles refrigerated in an airtight container, but let them come to room temperature before serving them.

Alan Roettinger
The Sweet Life/Agoura

 This page sponsored by Stephanie Damoman

CHART HOUSE RESTAURANT MUD PIE

Crush wafers and add butter. Mix well. Press into a 9" pie plate. Cover with soft coffee ice cream. Top with cold fudge sauce. (It helps to put the fudge sauce in the freezer for a while to make spreading easier.) Store the Mud Pie in the freezer for approximately 10 hours before serving.

Presentation: Slice the Mud Pie into eight portions and serve on chilled dessert plates. Top with whipped cream and diced almonds.

Chart House Restaurant
Malibu

4 1/2 ounce chocolate wafers
1/4 cup butter, melted
1 gallon coffee ice cream, soft
1 1/2 cups fudge sauce
whipped cream
diced almonds

ANNIE LAMPL TRIFLE

Annie Lampl lost her sight more than 25 years ago, and is now a counselor for the visually handicapped. Her friends and acquaintances stand in awe of her uncomplaining attitude and her famous desserts. This one is a favorite.

Cover the bottom of a 9" X 9" Pyrex pan with ladyfingers. Sprinkle with your favorite flavor liqueur and arrange fresh fruit on top. Cover completely. Prepare a package of French vanilla instant pudding and pour it over the fruit. Cover pudding with whipped cream and serve.

Annie Lampl

16-20 ladyfingers
fresh fruit in season
your favorite liqueur
1 package French Vanilla
    instant pudding
whipped cream

SALZBURGER NOCKEREN
FROM PENSION MIRABELL IN ST. WOLFGANG, AUSTRIA

3 eggs, separated
3 teaspoons flour
3 teaspoons powdered sugar
vanilla sugar

Mimi Kohner is the widow of the writer Frederick Kohner, world-famous for his "Gidget" books, movies and television series. The Kohners often came to Malibu for a swim and lunch, and Mimi, who is now 91, still comes for an occasional swim and walk. They appreciated the unspoiled nature of the beach and mountains, and the "Gidget" books often refer to Malibu.

Beat the egg whites, then add egg yolks and the other ingredients. Blend slowly. Place in a greased pan and bake about 8 minutes in a hot (375°) oven. Remove from oven. Cool. Sprinkle with vanilla sugar.

Mimi Kohner (Mother of Gidget)

A sampling of the Chocoholic's Nightmare Dessert Buffet includes, clockwise from top left, "Chocolate-Orange Cake With Raspberries", "Mocha Profiteroles", "Chocolate-Almond Tart", and "Chocolate Mint Truffles"

CHRISTINE'S COOKIES THAT BUILT A HOUSE

Christine Wuth and her husband Leo lost one home in the fire--one that was rented to tenants who were then invited to move in with them. The house in which they resided was half-burnt, so the two families continued to live there in half a house. When the workmen rebuilding the house lingered to rest, she ran and brought out these cookies.

1 cup (2 sticks) butter or Imperial margarine
1 cup dark brown sugar
1 cup white sugar

Cream together the first three ingredients.

Add remaining ingredients, mix together and drop by rounded teaspoonsful on greased baking sheets. Bake at 350° until golden brown (the time varies from 5 to 10 minutes). Let stand on the cookie sheet for a few seconds until you can remove in one piece with a spatula. Store air tight.

1/4 cup molasses
2 eggs
1 teaspoon baking soda
1/2 teaspoon salt
1/2 teaspoon baking powder
1/2 cup shredded coconut
1 cup wheat germ
1 cup whole wheat flour
1 cup chopped walnuts
1 12-ounce package chocolate chips

Christine Wuth

This page sponsored by Robin Steinberg

ATELIER DE CHOCOLAT'S CHOCOLATE TRUFFLE TORTE

With the hillsides aflame, the temperature well over 85° and thick black smoke and ash pouring in through every crack in our store, the immediate dilemma was just what to do with well over 500 pounds of assorted chocolates. The electricity had already gone out twice, and the air conditioning went along with it.

The call to evacuate having long been given, we conferred for a split second before doing the only thing possible. We threw caution, and our diets, to the wind and started eating. Our tummies, mouths and hands full, we bid a sad farewell to our little candy store for perhaps the last time and joined the others already helping those closer to the fire's path.

The building was spared but all of the chocolate was either melted or smoked beyond salvage. We conferred again, only for a second, before deciding: We love Malibu, we would start over, and so it was.

The next time you decide to throw caution, or your diet, to the wind, we highly recommend this sinfully rich chocolate torte.

1 pound semi-sweet dark
  chocolate
2 sticks unsalted butter
6 large eggs

In a large bowl, combine chocolate and butter. Melt in the microwave on high power stirring every 15 seconds. Remove when there are still a few lumps of chocolate and stir until fully melted.

In a large bowl, set over a pan of simmering water, heat the eggs, stirring constantly to prevent curdling, until just warm to the touch. Remove from the heat and beat, using a whisk until triple in volume and soft peaks form when the whisk is raised (about 5 minutes).

Using a rubber spatula, fold half the eggs into the chocolate mixture until almost incorporated. Fold in the remaining eggs until just blended and no streaks remain. Place in an 8" springform pan buttered and bottom lined with buttered parchment or wax paper.

Wrap the outside of the pan with a double layer of heavy duty foil to prevent seepage.

Place the pan in a 10" cake pan or roasting pan with 1" boiling water to bake at 425°. Bake 5 minutes, then cover with a piece of buttered foil and bake 10 more minutes.

The cake will look soft but this is how it should be. Cool on a rack for 45 minutes and cover with plastic wrap. Refrigerate until firm (about 3 hours) and serve with your favorite raspberry sauce or whipped cream (or both). Serve at room temperature.

Atelier de Chocolat
Malibu

PUMPKIN CAKE

1 29-ounce can pumpkin
4 eggs
1 12-ounce can evaporated milk
1 1/2 cups sugar
2 teaspoons cinnamon
1 teaspoon ground ginger
1/2 teaspoon nutmeg
1 package yellow cake mix
1 cup butter
1/2 cup chopped pecans

Lemon glaze:

1 cup powdered sugar
1 teaspoon lemon juice
1/2 teaspoon grated lemon rind
cream or half & half

Mix together the pumpkin, eggs, milk, sugar, cinnamon, ginger, and nutmeg.

Pour into a 9" X 15" or 9" X 13" pan that has been sprayed with Pam®. Sprinkle top with dry cake mix and then drizzle melted butter over the top. Sprinkle nuts on top.

Bake 350° for 1 hour. Serve with whipped cream or lemon glaze.

For lemon glaze, combine sugar, lemon juice, and grated lemon rind. Add just enough cream to make glaze slightly runny. Drizzle over top and sides of cake.

Louise Logan

FIREHOUSE PEARS

This recipe seems most appropriate for a cookbook which will commemorate the Malibu Fire of '93.

Combine the sugar, egg, butter, rum, peel, and ginger. Refrigerate 3 to 4 hours to allow flavors to meld. Fold in the whipped cream. Peel, halve and core the pears. Arrange pear halves on plates and top with the sauce. Serves 8

Gustav and Betty Ullner

I cup powdered sugar
I egg, well beaten
3 tablespoons melted butter
2 tablespoons rum
I teaspoon grated lemon peel
1/4 teaspoon ginger
I cup whipping cream, whipped

8 Comice pears, cooked or canned

PINEAPPLE DUMP CAKE

Pour cherry pie filling and crushed pineapple into a 9" X 13" pan. Mix well, and spread out evenly.

Crumble dry cake mix over the top. Pour melted butter over the top of cake mix. Crumble nuts and coconut over top.

Bake at 325° for I hour. Cool and serve with whipped cream.

Dorothy Wood

I can cherry pie filling
I 20-ounce can crushed pineapple
I box yellow cake mix
I cup butter or margarine, melted
I cup grated coconut
I cup chopped pecans

BROWN DERBY RESTAURANT CHIFFON CAKE

2 1/2 cups sifted cake flour
   (Softasilk)
1 1/2 cups sugar
3 teaspoons baking powder
1 teaspoon salt
1/2 cup Wesson or Mazola oil
5 medium-sized egg yolks,
   unbeaten
3/4 cup cold water
2 teaspoons vanilla
grated rind from 1 lemon
   (optional)
7 or 8 egg whites
1/2 teaspoon cream of tartar

Sift flour onto paper, then measure. In a mixing bowl, sift together the flour, sugar, baking powder, and salt. Make a well in the center of the ingredients and add, one at a time, the oil, egg yolks, water, vanilla, and lemon rind. Beat with a wooden spoon until smooth.

Place egg whites and cream of tartar in large mixing bowl and whip until whites form very stiff peaks. Do not underbeat, as this must be much stiffer than for angel food or meringue.

Pour egg-yolk mixture gradually over whipped egg whites, gently folding batter into whites with rubber scraper or heavy spoon until mixture is just blended. DO NOT STIR.

Pour into ungreased 9" pans immediately, dividing mixture in two. Bake in a 350° oven for 45 to 50 minutes. Cake is done when top springs back when lightly touched.

Remove pan from oven and immediately turn upside down, resting the edges on two other pans. Allow the cake to hang, free of the table, until cold. Loosen from sides with spatula, turn pan over, and hit edge sharply on table to loosen.

When cool, ice chiffon cake with Brown Derby Grapefruit Cheese Frosting.

Beat cream cheese until fluffy. Add lemon juice and rind. Gradually blend in sugar. Beat until well blended. Add coloring, Crush several of the grapefruit sections to measure 2 teaspoons. Blend into frosting.

Spread frosting on bottom half of cake. Top with several grapefruit sections. Cover with second layer. Frost top and sides, and garnish with remaining grapefruit sections.

Peggy Cobb
Brown Derby Restaurant

Brown Derby Grapefruit Cheese Frosting:

2 6-ounce packages cream
    cheese, softened
2 teaspoons lemon juice
1 teaspoon grated lemon rind
3/4 cup powdered sugar, sifted
6 to 8 drops yellow food
    coloring
Sections from 1 large or 2 small
    fresh grapefruit, peeled,
    seeded, and membranes
    removed

 This page sponsored by Stan & Barbara Krasnoff

CHOCOLATY CHOCOLATE PIE

I stick butter or margarine
I 1/2 cups crumbled chocolate
    wafers (or Oreo® cookies)

I 6-ounce package semi-sweet
    chocolate bits
2 tablespoons vanilla
3 eggs
I 1/4 cups whipping cream,
    whipped or I carton dessert
    whipped topping

Melt the butter and mix with crumbled cookies. Put mixture into a buttered pie plate. Press to form shell. Bake in 375° oven for 3 minutes. Cool.

Make the filling by melting the chocolate bits over hot water. Beat in one whole egg and two yolks, one at a time. Add the vanilla. Beat the remaining two egg whites until stiff, and fold into the chocolate mixture. Then fold in the whipped cream or whipped dessert topping.

Spoon mixture into pie shell and chill for at least 5 or 6 hours. You may top with more whipped cream and chocolate shavings if desired.

This is a non-violent recipe, but everyone fights for seconds!

Serves 8

Ellen Copeland

NEW ORLEANS RICE PUDDING

In the November 2nd firestorms, I lost recipes from my great-grandmother, mother, and other family members in Louisiana. I recently went to New Orleans to retrieve a few, but this one stuck in my head as it was a favorite of my daughters Heather and Vanessa while growing up in Malibu over the last 25 years.

We will rebuild on Big Rock, and since I am expecting my first grandchild in February '95, I expect to begin again making the traditional things my girls always enjoyed.

The day of the fire, I went off to work leaving a frozen meatloaf to defrost for dinner. I guess it was a little over-cooked! We never got back in to check on it.

In a bowl, whip the eggs and then add all other ingredients.

Place pudding in a heavy casserole dish and bake at 400° for 10 minutes. Lower the oven temperature to 350° and continue baking for 50 minutes longer.

June Rickett

3 eggs
1 tablespoon vanilla
3/4 stick melted butter
1 can evaporated milk
1/4 cup raisins
2 tart apples, sliced
2 1/2 cups cooked, cold long
   grain rice
3/4 cup sugar

LEMON ICE CREAM

3/4 cup lemon juice
2 tablespoons grated lemon rind
2 cups granulated sugar
2 cups whipping cream,
    unwhipped
2 cups sour cream, mixed
    slightly

As a fire survivor, I am more than happy to contribute this favorite recipe. It is not only delicious, but very simple to make. I have very happy memories of picking the lemons from my backyard tree and whipping up this dessert for family and friends.

Last November 2nd, we lost that lemon tree, plus our home and much more. But my son-in-law, who was helping us throw what we could into the cars, ran into my office and spotted my battered recipe file box on the shelf. He grabbed it, and because of him, I still have the hundreds of recipes collected over many years. And I expect to have a lemon tree again soon, too!

In a large bowl, whisk together juice, rind, and sugar. Slowly add whipping cream and then the sour cream, mixing well. Pour into a serving dish and freeze about 6 hours or until firm.

Lore Klein

FOURTH OF JULY PIE

Preheat oven to 450°.

Work butter, lard and flour first with fingers and then lightly rotate between palms of hands, making a well. Gradually pour in cold water and sugar.

Use index finger to stir liquid with flour in a spiral fashion, gradually moving to outer well. Dough should be soft enough to gather into a ball, but should not stick to fingers. Allow dough to rest refrigerated from 2 to 36 hours. Cover with damp, wrung-out cloth for shorter time period, but cover with foil if leaving for longer amount of time.

When ready to assemble pie, roll out dough for two crusts for a 9" pie pan. Place one crust in a pie pan and cover with foil. Weight down with beans and bake until a light golden brown--about 10 minutes. Remove from oven.

Sprinkle sugar, flour and lemon juice over the berries and stir gently until well blended. Turn fruit into shell of the pie. Dot with 1 to 2 tablespoons butter.

Cover pie with a full crust that has been well-pricked, or a lattice top crust. Bake pie at 450° 10 minutes. Reduce the heat to 350° and bake 35-40 minutes longer until golden brown.

Alyson Cook

Crust:

1/2 cup chilled butter
3 tablespoons lard or vegetable shortening
2 cups all-purpose flour
1/2 teaspoon salt

5 to 6 tablespoons cold water
3 tablespoons sugar

Filling:

4 1/2 cups mixed berries
3/4 to 1 cup sugar
1/4 cup all-purpose flour
1 1/2 tablespoons lemon juice

VANILLA SUNSET

I pint non-fat vanilla frozen
  yogurt
I cup whole, unsweetened
  frozen strawberries
I cup whole, unsweetened
  frozen raspberries or
  blackberries
2 tablespoons white sugar
2 tablespoons Grand Marnier
  (optional)
I tablespoon Droste Dutch
  cocoa powder
4 sprigs fresh mint

A low-fat dessert creation by fitness trainer Paul Kiers.

Chill 4 ice cream bowls in the freezer.

Place a scoop of yogurt in each bowl and return to the freezer.

In a medium, preheated saucepan, combine frozen berries, sugar, and optional Grand Marnier. Cook over medium heat 6 to 8 minutes, stirring frequently. Cook an additional 2 minutes on low heat to thicken if necessary.

Remove the bowls of yogurt from the freezer and sift a small amount of Dutch cocoa powder on each. Remove the berries from the heat and place a scoop on top of each bowl.

Garnish with mint and serve immediately.

Paul Kiers

Acknowledgments

I am deeply grateful to my family for sharing me, understanding and supporting me in this project: my husband Jeff, my gift of life and the best friend anyone could ever have; my sons, Ryan and Chad, for being the wonderful young men they are; my mother, for showing me the love of entertaining; and my grandma, for being the best cook.

How does one find the right words to thank a group of special people who have been so generous with their time, energy and talents?

To *"The Image Maker"* Beverly Hammond, our publisher and unofficial managing editor, who managed to publish this book against all odds...and ends. Bev pulled together our recipes, vignettes, photos and more and designed them into the handsome, professional work we handed over to our printer with pride.

To Gina Burrell, my right-hand assistant, recipe tester, part-time secretary, friend, always there.

To Ann Fulton, editor and proof-reader extraordinaire, who contributed countless hours.

To Louis Hill, our treasure of a treasurer and tracker of Friends and Sponsors.

To Mary Lou Siemons, more than a dear friend, who typed all of our recipes from endless scraps of paper.

To Selwyn Yosslowitz of *Marmalade Café*, for his gusto, creativity, and practical spirit.

To Alan Roettinger, wonderful cook and philosopher, who wrote reams of beautiful dessert recipes, then reluctantly, but congenially, edited them to the nub.

To precious friend Donnovan Field, who kindly but firmly kept reminding me of our deadlines.

To the very talented Bobby Duron and Linda Conrad who elevated our book with their exquisite color photography.

To Rabbi Levi Cunin and *Chabad of Malibu* for believing in our project and negotiating with *Quebecor Printing* so that this book might be put into print.

To Jeanette Farr of *Bambu* for her commitment to the community and incredible energy in providing endless meals to firefighters last November, and who allowed us to meet and plan this project at her restaurant.

To all the wonderful cooks and restaurants who submitted recipes, along with our Book, Page Sponsors, and Friends who supported us. This book would never have become a reality without your help.

To Hayden Finley, who connected us with the Greater Malibu Disaster Recovery Project and elicited their involvement and support.

To Howard Spanier of *Mail Boxes, Etc.*, who never stopped giving. He is such an asset to our community.

To artist Laddie John Dill who graciously allowed us to use one of his artworks as the cover for our cookbook, reflecting the cyclical energies of earth, sea, and fire.

To Fini Littlejohn, the artistic angel who created our angelic logo.

To Chef Kevin Ripley and Pam Brunson of *Granita* restaurant for graciously arranging our recipe photography session there.

To *The Prince's Table* in Pacific Palisades for their impressive china and John Cosentino of *Malibu Florist*, for their beautiful flowers seen in our photography.

To *Malibu Surfside News* publisher and editor Anne Soble, for including us among all the non-profit community endeavors she continuously supports.

To sculptress Arlene Waxman and her husband Jerry, for hosting our cookbook premiere at their estate, surrounded by Arlene's moving sculpture, *"Remnants of the '93 Firestorm"*.

To Harvey Baskin of *Geoffrey's/Malibu* restaurant, for sharing his marketing expertise and supporting us in our fund-raising efforts.

To Marlene Adler Marks for her insightful, thought-provoking introduction to our book.

To Bill Edmonds, whose firestorm cloud photo reflects our upbeat theme of hope and renewal.

To all the recipe testers at *Let's Get Cookin'* in Westlake Village who checked the quality of our recipes.

To Shari Diamond, Dede Goodman, and Marla Obari whose tragic losses inspired the concept of *Malibu's Cooking Again.*

To Karen and Arnold York, publishers of *The Malibu Times*, who took their own personal heartbreak and selflessly channeled it outward to create Operation Recovery. This support group reached out and united Malibu's fire victims, provided them with a network of professional advisors, helped them to view themselves not as victims but survivors, and gave them shoulders to laugh and cry on. *Malibu's Cooking Again* is proud to be a contributor to their effort and to those who experienced losses in the fires.

Lastly, to all the people of Malibu who make living here so special. May we always be there for one another.

-- *Cathy Rogers*

Recipe Index